IMAGES OF WOMEN

Images of Women

an anthology of contemporary women's poetry

Edited by Myra Schneider

and Dilys Wood

for Second Light Network

ARROWHEAD
PRESS

First published 2006 by
Arrowhead Press

70 Clifton Road, Darlington
Co. Durham, DL1 5DX
Tel: (01325) 260741

Typeset in 10pt Laurentian by
Arrowhead Press

Email: editor@arrowheadpress.co.uk
Website: http://www.arrowheadpress.co.uk

ISBN-10: 1-904852-14-9
ISBN-13: 978-1-904852-14-8

Second Light Network acknowledges the financial assistance
of Arts Council England.

Arrowhead Press is a member of
Independent Northern Publishers.

Printed by Athenaeum Press, Gateshead, Tyne and Wear.

Contents

Section 4

Section 5

PART FIVE   LOVE RELATIONSHIPS

PART SIX   RELATIONSHIPS

Section 1

Section 2

Section 3

Section 4

PART SEVEN   INNER SELF AND IMAGINATION

Introduction

For centuries the images of women in poetry, drama, fiction and the visual arts were created by men. Women's representations of women are now making a strong impact in all the arts. Part of this is the exploration and questioning of stereotypes and traditional roles. Beginning with the Sylvia Plath generation, women poets have written frankly self-revealing poetry marked by a new assertiveness – and this is only one aspect of how they explore their world.

We have aimed to reflect women's aspirations not only in the contents of the anthology but in the way we solicited material and let this shape the book. Through advertisements in poetry magazines and by other forms of outreach we invited women poets, including those in the Second Light Network, to submit as much work about women as they wished, whether written by themselves or by other living poets writing in English. The response was enormous and we have read many moving, angry, tender, humorous and imaginative poems.

The great strength of women's poetry now is its increasing diversity and ambition. In addition to the many personal poems we received, a key focus was the social and political status of women. We chose poems which were not solely a rant against men but those reflecting the global scale of denigration and violence, confinement to limited roles and, sometimes, mistreatment of women by women. These ranged from wry comments to outcries against severe abuse. The extent to which women may still be considered inadequate and even tainted by their female biology – and how this saps confidence – came across clearly. In contrast, we have included many celebratory poems about determined, feisty women who 'buck the trend' and offer a lead to others.

Images of Women covers the gamut of women's lives and relationships in seven sections. The final part, 'Inner Life and Imagination' is, in one sense, our attempt to turn the rest of book on its head. In much of the anthology the poets are precise chroniclers of their own and other women's lives. Rich detail, wit, reflection and the confrontation of emotion are involved. However, we have chosen to conclude with work focussed, not on daily lives, but on women's creativity and spirituality. These final poems draw on mythology, recreate the distant past, use images, symbols and the surreal to explore feelings and perceptions of self. 'The Badge' by Hilary Llewellyn-Williams draws us into a vision:

Finding myself after nights of grief and dread
in a room full of rainy light
knife in my hand, no-one can do this for me,
I prepare for the ceremony

I am about to join the community
of those who have removed and replaced their heads.

Of course, throughout the anthology the poems reflect the power of the imagination and one of the earliest in the book, Isobel Thrilling's 'Birth of an Escapologist', is the portrait of a young girl at a stuffy tea-party who takes off into another world:

Wings of curtains drift over
this new creature
assembling its natal flight,
the skill to release herself to the sky.

It has been a privilege to bring together these poems, which express the range of women's experiences, attitudes and aspirations.

Myra Schneider   Dilys Wood

Preface

This is a book that has been waiting to be written since, perhaps, the nineteen-seventies, when women at last began to play a serious part in the world of poetry. These images of women are images *by* women, constructed out of twenty-first century consciousness, unmediated by the male gaze.

It's fatal, of course, to generalise, and first impressions are often unreliable – and yet, what strikes one so strongly in this anthology is the *absence of pretentiousness*. Why is this the case with women who write poetry? How do they manage it? Perhaps it's because women, somehow more deftly than men, contrive to combine a hands-on approach to their material with a detached perspective. Their experience offers too little time, too many demands, for them to elaborate theories or philosophies that aren't firmly rooted in the tried and tested everyday. And so we have the close attention to detail that brings poems to life; sets alight the subtle moments of change and development, the sudden insights into the responsibility, courage, hope, violence, discontinuity and contradiction that lie at the heart of women's experience.

The editors have wisely resisted the temptation to try to fit all the poems into a strictly chronological framework. Initially we do travel with the years from childhood to old age, but there are other rich seams to mine, other aspects of life that women deal with particularly well – portraits, for example, or relationships, or work. Not for these writers the jibes of thirty years ago, about women's writing being exclusively about menstruation and childbirth: everything is here, and the picture is of a warm and rich humanity, not an embattled gender protest.

So here we have children and their inventiveness; self-conscious teenagers, *scared at the dance-hall*; their loneliness, coming to terms with their bodies, with boys, with danger; young women before and after pregnancy and their sense of *general wear and tear and age*, their joy in the present and their fear of the future, their children growing mysterious and strange.

Perhaps it's not surprising that, though these poems are generally sharp and unsentimental, it's middle age and later years that offer the most scope for wit. Women aren't given to self-pity. There are, instead, diatribes about women who *work out*, and women who dye their hair, poems about those who are *knocking on*, who have the guts to explore their *varicose wirings* and their breasts *like ineptly cooked Yorkshire puddings*. There's no looking back regretfully, either: here's a last wish –

Before I go down to the ferryman
All set for the final journey
I'll find me a Cork or Kerry man
From Droom or Ballyvourney...

and *motherhood*? Whoops! – that's something to be *got rid of*, in a great clearing-out of life, along with the collections of elephants and the plants and everything else, leaving *room, time, space*. Portraits and the world of work also provide rich territory for these writers. But there is no sentimentality, and certainly no clichés. As well as to mothers (a tough lot, these, on the whole) there are affectionate and touching tributes to mothers-in-law and stepmothers, and to much-loved maids. There's a brief witty picture of a madam in a sex shop (who counts the crotchless panties in the same way she'd count oven gloves); a soliloquy, as she watches the tourists, by Sheela-na-gig; a marvellous monologue *The Wife of Bafa* from Nigeria. Nothing is predictable: *Filling the Kettle* involves cutting through the Arctic ice; and an eighty-five-year-old writer is discovered to be writing about Tree Frogs in Sarawak. Work isn't hoovering – it's rude jokes in the carrot field; it's digging a *cellophaned mitt / into the spirogyra of necks like willies* in the chicken factory; it's a woman sitting in the dark of the Shetlands, weaving *mist in her fingers* into the mysterious *white poems* of lace.

I've read it all from cover to cover, and I'd happily sit down and read it all over again.

U A Fanthorpe

Part 1

Life Cycle

Overblown Roses

She held one up, twirling it in her hand
as if to show me how the world began
and ended in perfection. I was stunned.
How could she make a rose so woebegone,
couldn't silk stand stiff? And how could a child,
otherwise convinced of her mother's taste,
know what to think? *It's overblown*, she smiled,
I love roses when they're past their best.

'Overblown roses', the words swam in my head,
making sense as I suddenly saw afresh
the rose now, the rose ahead: where a petal
clings to a last breath; where my mother's flesh
and mine, going the same way, may still
be seen as beautiful, if these words are said.

Mimi Khalvati

1

Seeing that Woman

Seeing that woman walk across a field,
I remembered your blue wool coat,
the warm smell of it the day you left.

Blue-coated, she walks diagonally, alone.
Behind her, rows of blank windows.
I don't have the feeling anyone's waiting.

The train I'm in gathers speed and something
in the light has changed, so that now I see
myself out there too, sliding along beside her.

Of course, she doesn't look up: only I
can see my ghost, so weirdly seated,
floating over the grass, but gazing away

from her towards the woman in the train.
It's comic. Except that now I'm crying,
as if I could reach out to hold the coat

and see again the double seams yours had
on the shoulder, see small hands gripping
the blue, bunching it, hear myself crying.

Anne Cluysenaar

Birth of an Escapologist

This bowl of hyacinths transmits
a blue pulse,
scent heavy with thunders,

a bruise,
a thug at the throat,
the child is drugged with boredom,
slugged by sweetness.

The afternoon
swings its cosh and elderly aunts,
avid yet powdery,
flutter their bones, ecstatic
among the tea-cups,
sleeves rustle like membranes.

She has lost the power to hear
their voices,
just a needle of sound can stab
the silence
wound round her head;
the air wraps her in hot velvet.

She is living a fairy-tale,
the chrysalis of a child in thrall,
she must weave
her own colours, make inner fabric.

Wings of curtains drift over
this new creature
assembling its natal flight,
the skill to release herself to the sky.

Isobel Thrilling

Dreams

In the dark suburb where Daddy shouted
we invented our own island.
It floated between our beds.
You were the fairy queen and I a fat man,
messenger to the outside world.
We were alone, anchored in one imagination,
connected by a pact we understood, but never voiced.
We scooped our island out of the night tide,
it saved us from the shouts that flooded floor-boards,
unhinged doors, dug out holes.
When it was time to go you sang u bell.
Then sleep leaned over us, hauled up our island
into a net of spray and stars.

Susan Skinner

Moon

There was no tide here
just stones
sitting in the river
and a mermaid's comb
which marked the magic
of my coming

a thatched shed
covering the heads of yams
became our doll's house
where we played
Mamma and Pappa
nakedly

touch mi
tell mi

'yah so Mr Finnegan,
yah so sah,
but yah so no sweet
like a yah so sah'

the brutal entry
of my mother
brought guilt
and suddenly I understood
at six
how clothes came into the garden

Oh Eve
Oh innocent one

Jean Binta Breeze

Erma's Search

She climbs the hill, scarlet face and rasping breath,
trickly sweat all down her neck,
a crimson woolly jumper scratches
under pitching sun.

Here's the child whose mother planted
red hot pokers shoulder high
and blood red roses lashing spite –

who never knew the comfort of her name,
tagged as Tom or Roy
she might have been a boy.

No friends, no school, no holidays or cards,
no-one ever called;
beyond the world lay foreigners and danger –
'There are plenty who will harm,' her mother said.

Near the top, she gasps and tumbles,
sunstroke sick –

this child compelled by quest
obsessed by tales of pagan days
and kingdoms drowned in sand.

In the jar she carries,
black flies seethe and buzz.

Mandy Pannett

Alice and Hilda

They were twins in my class at school.
I sometimes think of them when I'm ashamed
of myself: dark-haired girls with straight-cut fringes
like characters in Enid Blyton stories.

At their house they showed me the lavvies outside,
behind a high brick wall like those at school.
I forget what happened next but as I peed
Hilda shoved Alice into the door screaming

that she wet the bed.
Alice, her cheeks scarlet, huddled against the wall.
I stumbled forward, dragging up my pants,
yelling again and again: *So do I! So do I!*

Joan Poulson

Deadnettle

Sprawled under the hedge he snaps
the thin necks of deadnettle,
pinches the white sac, squirts
nectar into my mouth.
A small sweet promise on the tongue.

I run home in the heat. The smell
of melting tar, a stickiness underfoot.
The house whirrs and stutters with the machine.
She urges a small red dress to the needle.

She stops, examines me, stretches
to tug a snag of stickybud from my hair.
Be a good girl. She takes up the cloth

and snaps the thread on her teeth. *Won't you?*

Jean Sprackland

The Magma Room

Then his window turned to quartz crystal
and his curtains to rock.
I was back in the magma chamber
of my childhood
           in my father's bedroom.

He'd punched a crater in my chest
and we'd both fallen in
then resurfaced, burnished,
the heat almost melting my bones,
the sheets glowing red, then
           bursting into flame.

My face pressed into the lava pillow
would always leave a mask
as he pushed further into me.
And when I tried to pull away,
the stone face I now had,
stared at the ceiling
           and saw it bubble.

My long black hair
flowed down me in rivers of fire
which he kept stroking and twisting
           until the roots tore.

I slipped into a molten darkness,
down to a white core
where I was numbed.
A doctor woke me
on the cool kitchen table.

Over forty years have passed
since I buried that night
under clouds of volcanic ash.

But when you ask me what I remember –
all I say is his smell,
     like a stone lining in my nostrils.

Pascale Petit

Partobar

I creaked towards sunlight, my new boots stiff
on the barn floor. I knew Partobar was saddled up
and angry, gnashing the bit. Neither of us wanted this:
the authority of the crop in my shaking hand,
the smell of manure and leather, fresh hay
stinging my eyes – they expected me to ride him,
part Quarter, part Arabian, his coat like copper in the sun.

As I entered the paddock he watched me,
head lowered, ears twitching, the other girls
watching too, their blonde ponytails
neat down their backs, their jackets perfect,
the instructor in the corner, arms folded – all waiting
for me to fail. I came up beside him, lifted my foot
to the stirrup, swung myself up by the reins.

At first the air seemed thin, my head
was throbbing, but as I tugged, Partobar started moving
as if we had come to some secret arrangement.
I began to relax, my body doing exactly what it should,
the air around us buzzing, his hooves in rhythm
with my every move. We galloped, the symmetry
of the paddock breaking into stripes of speed.

Then without warning Partobar bucked.
I started falling sideways, still grasping the reins,
a rush of air, a thump as I hit the ground,
dirt and blood in my mouth, my head a bell clap
inside the hard hat. I felt rays of heat
in the paddock, the whisper of girls, their giggles,
while Partobar circled me, bobbing his head.

After that, it was always the same; the taste
of my humiliation, Partobar towering above.
Finally, I let braver girls trot around the field,
chins up, asses out, proper deportment for a horse
and for life. I see them now at parties – you can always tell
a woman who had a horse thing; hair still long,
good skin, that giggle. And the men whinny approval.

I am still creaking through the barn,
my breasts like acorns beneath the vest,
the velvet jacket clinging to my skinny arms,
knowing he is waiting at the other end:
Partobar, all confidence, all sixteen hands, ready
to conquer me again, his golden haunches
streaming with sweat, his nostrils flared.

Tamar Yoseloff

2

Coming of Age

On Southwold beach. It isn't the shout
of the boys but the distance calling.
Eleven. Walking away. A salt lick
and the cling of cotton to her thighs.
Granules: grey, yellow, mica, through her toes.

She treads unevenly through silver sheets,
flowers of foam, the shingle cutting her feet:
first blood. Fragments of shell in her fingers,
cockles, pink tellins, fanned ribs,
her hands shut carefully round their secrets.

In the bud of her body a cherry
is swelling red dreams. She straightens,
as if a woman hovers in her frame,
a bow of light in her wavering stem,
its slow pulse pushing to the sun.

A backward glance to the island
of her family. Distances greater than sand.
Their three heads clustered over driftwood,
a pen-and-ink miniature. The east wind
tugs at her skirt, turning the page.

Lynne Wycherley

Photographs

At twelve I didn't like my own face, because
my eyes were huge and open as a dog's,
and I wanted slitty eyes like Virginia Mayo.

Photographs show me laughing and healthy,
with wide shoulders and strong wrists that could take me
up the pear tree to the highest boughs.

Between these brown card covers adolescence
stirs. 'Oh Daddy,' I asked once
'why aren't I prettier?' He was kindly but embarrassed.

Now I look back on photographs of that girl
as if I were already some ginger-haired ghost
visiting a sepia world of strangers,

and among so many faces I like most
her laughter lines, strong nose and windblown hair.
And if I could fly back I should whisper to her

where she stands, painted and scared in the dance hall
setting out her sexual wares: What you
think of as disadvantages will bring you through.

Elaine Feinstein

Their Words
from: Sheba and Solomon

A dark winter day. The end of an afternoon.
A young girl sits in the empty school library
reading *Solomon's Song*. She thinks of an orchard:
almond / apple / etrog / pomegranate / fig.
She stares down at the whorled grain of the table,
the same pattern there on her fingertips,
and reads again: 'My beloved is unto me as
a cluster of camphire in the vineyards of En-Gedi.'
She sees a fountain, its jets and conduits,
the marble basin carved with rampant lions
and dragon-headed cherubim. Around it
grow flowers and spices: crocus / roses / lilies.
'I am my beloved's, and my beloved is mine:
he feedeth among the lilies.' The words disturb
and excite. Myrrh / spikenard / frankincense.
Her whole body goes icy-hot, imagining
that caress. Under sleeves and stockings,
at the back of her neck, the soft hairs lift.

Ruth Fainlight

Women's Blood

Burn the soiled ones in the boiler,
my mother told me, showing me how to hook
the loops of gauze-covered wadding pads
onto an elastic belt, remembering
how my grandmother had given her
strips of rag she'd had to wash out
every month for herself: the grandmother
who had her chair by the boiler,
who I loved but was plotting to murder
before she murdered my mother, or my mother –
shaking, sobbing, hurling plates and cups,
screaming she wished she'd never been born,
screeching 'Devil!' and 'Witch!' –
murdered her. I piled up the pads
until the smell satisfied me
it was the smell of a corpse.
'How could you do such a thing?'
my mother asked, finding them
at the bottom of the wardrobe
where the year before she'd found
a cache of navy-blue knickers
stained with the black jelly clots
I thought were my wickedness
oozing out of me.

Vicki Feaver

Landrover

The Landrover rattles and clanks in the heat
She likes being high seeing over the tops
of the hedges into fields, brown scorched patches,
sheep looking for shadow, sucking sparse grass listlessly.

She likes his slow lazy words, the way he makes her feel grown up.
He stops by the river where the fish swim
cool and languid under the still water,
tips of green shaded trees burning in the hot sun.

His face is threaded with broken red veins
tiny worms crawling, grey slate eyes staring.
Her skin itches. He starts to sing, big bass voice
rolling out over the fields unafraid.

With fluid smooth confidence he touches
her breasts lightly; she flinches.
Unbuttons her shirt pinching skin,
laughing, 'they'll grow darling.'

He smells of beer and stale aftershave.
She is frightened of his brown swarthy hands.
A car drones, carefully inching its way toward them.
She cries softly; 'slut' he drawls.

She goes to the river, swims deep under the bridge.
Shame seeps into her bones,
aches through the hours,
binds her tight in the blind empty days.

Catherine Whittaker

Anorectic

in her kitchen, a tiny set of scales
calibrated in milligrams, in her bathroom
her three times a day electric weighing machine
she can calculate calories exactly, how many
in two lettuce leaves, how many in a halved tomato,
a peeled apple, a forbidden banana, a yoghurt.
This is her knowledge kept close, private
far from prying, probing eyes. Yes, she can hear
the visitors below but will not join them, not for lunch,
not for dinner, not for anything. She hates women
their constant talk of ectomies of all kinds,
of diets, children, problems down below, problems.
She runs at night in the streets to escape. Free as a bird,
light as a bird, she dreams of soaring back to the place
she scarcely remembers, utterly safe, under no scrutiny,
the perfect child, pale, thin and bloodless as a crucifixion.

Jacqueline Brown

Children's Ward

This friend of mine was 15
when she stuffed herself with painkillers,
made her ears ring, her head swim, her brain choke,
and then was sick and sick, emptied herself
of the ghosts that munched away at her,
threw up a bit of crushed white paste, it doesn't take much,
the acid in her mouth a blessing, an amazing feat
of escapology, her first real glimpse of mortality
and immortality. Because she was not yet 16,
they put her in the children's ward at the hospital,
where we found her the next day,
lost among colouring books and toy musical instruments.
We were the same age. We didn't know what to do
and we had brought too many words, too many
presents and sweets, and the nurses disliked us,
and our laughter, which we only meant as medicine.
So many of us try to die, they lose patience.
I remember lying on the floor, investigating whether I
could levitate a malteser, make it hover above my lips
by blowing my breath steadily out. Desperate to entertain,
to bring, with the silly and surreal, some kind of comfort.
She had gone so far and it was over so quickly,
out the same day, one social worker session, and
back home. Her mother, desolate in a Disney sweatshirt,
invited us back and bought ice cream.
Haagen-Dazs and videos and the hospital smell lingering.
The world's strangest party. Sometimes people
just don't know what to do. And if sometimes
they try to fill the gap with small talk, evasion,
sentimentality, grant them tolerance.
All we can do is understand, or, failing that, forgive.
Make your forgiveness huge and encompassing. Remember that
sometime you will be without maps or boundaries,
without up or down, lost in a storm.

Jane Kinninmont

Princess

You came rocking back from the south,
hanging off the seat, trying
to be still, be good for mummy
who'd known just the man
to right your little error.

And you sang nursery rhymes all night
to your pretty rosebud wall
to your glass and china frogs
to the photos of yourself.
You sang until the words came wrong

and then you clenched your knees
and cried and promised never never.
She hushed you, showed you in her mirror
mirror that connects how this begins
with how it sometimes never ends.

She cleared the room, cradled you
until you woke, then brought red wine
to build you up and celebrate
a close scrape, a lucky break, and you,
Princess, as good as gold, as good as new.

Ann Sansom

The Blue Darkness

I'm reading *Bavarian Gentians* and it's not death I see, or
      Persephone's shotgun marriage in the fields of Enna. No.

It's the long coarse throats of gentians gross as pitcher
      plants, lapped in the rangy grass of La Chartreuse.

Jos is wearing indigo jeans, Bavarian gentian jeans. His
      presence is marinading my innards to a soup. I lust
      luxuriously and on the quiet. He has no idea.

There are five of us on the valley road to La Chartreuse,
      down near the riverbed where the woodsorrel flowers
      are pale as shock, and forget-me-nots shake dull stars
      into the stream. Only the gentians hold the deep dye
      colourfast in their grassy spools.

A thin fire runs through my limbs. I am paler than woodland
      grass, paler than sorrel. I am seventeen.

Catherine Byron

Gone

Each touch, my skin giggles
under your finger tips. My teeth
want to feel each tender morsel; your toes,
your ears, your willing lips, the nape
of your neck. Each touch and we are gone
deeper into each other

      until suffocated in sweetness this attic
room with its slow heat, its pillow
of air that it is not air that rises smooth
into our lungs as we breathe the burn
of each other, as we taste the sweat
that tastes of nothing else but water
that rises from the earth, that holds us
in some timeless place all afternoon.

Helen Ivory

3

Fire Child

On Beltane, an ancient festival, women
trying to conceive would run between fires.

I thread myself between twin fires
allowing one breath for the path.
My body is singed and smoked –
still I bathe in ashes and soot.

Other women bloom into summer
picking swathes of white hawthorn.
My blossom is the flames,
a slow-burning blaze within me.

There is nothing I will not try:
one night I walk barefoot
over red-hot stones, my arms a cradle.

Anne Ryland

The Unborn

Completely self-absorbed,
they're poring over plans
for a long journey
with their checklist
of fingers and toes to hand.

Buddhas in the making
who look beyond this world:
they've swum dark seas,
heard hollow tom toms,
and moved on.

They cold-shoulder me.
I'm not deep enough
to fathom, and my desire
to cuddle them
is beyond their dreams.

Jill Townsend

Allowing the Animal

After your father had come (I hadn't – didn't know
such a thing, not then) I lay on the blue-green
looped synthetic carpet pedalling air.
I even tried to hold a shoulderstand
to the count of nine, I was so keen
your egg should meet your sperm.
Would gravity help? Someone
had said so, thought that our problem might be
that your father's spunk ran out
too soon. Was I abnormally slopey?

I'd always been good at exams
and I only failed my driving test once
before passing. Why couldn't I get this right?
No one could say I wasn't serious,
stuck on this bathroom carpet between the bath and the door
checking my chart: yes, this was
the day of the temperature rise.
It was all thermometer and graphs
standing like puzzled fairies round your conception

like it was hospital ironmongery round your birth.
Suddenly now I wish that when you were born
I had taken your unshawled body into my unrobed arms
and licked you clean. I wish I had tasted
your vernix, our waters, our blood,
and then bitten the quicting cord in two.
Why don't we lick our babies?
Why didn't I lick you?

Catherine Byron

The Ringing Chamber

I was four months gone –
my breasts already tender
against the bell-ropes;

we were ringing quarter-peals,
the sun flooding the bell-chamber,
the dust rippling between the joists

when the child quickened,
fluttered against the changes;
and suddenly through the clerestory

I saw that colder quickening –
random, reciprocal –
cloudshadow

and the flaxfield
like water under the wind.

Pauline Stainer

Psalm

O Night and Silence,
        why should I complain?

For though I am empty, and pale as veal,
        surely your servants are good.

I came here bloody, and they undressed me;
they cast aside my clothes,
        for they were soiled.

Into my veins
they pushed their merciful darkness.
Like a branch of its blossoms,
        they scraped me clean.

All night, they have watched over me;
they have lifted the sheets
        and marked my loss.

They tell me my loss is normal:
      yea, I am filled with statistics.

Hour by hour, their kindness drips:
      water and salt, the smaller mercies.

O Great Indifference,
      to whom should I complain?

Joanne Limburg

Pregnancy

A country world, a rooted death
embracing stones. No need to wash
this air is white and pure.

The season shrinks, I swell.
As willows moult I venture leaves,
people this rustic limbo with my dreams.

An infant body battens on my own,
disturbs and conquers sleep,
lives richly like a maggot in fresh meat.

Waiting, I wish to die. That corpse
the moon unveils should be my own,
bared fangs and bloodied snout that bite the sky.

Valerie Clarke

Poem for a Daughter

'I think I'm going to have it,'
I said, joking between pains.
The midwife rolled competent
sleeves over corpulent milky arms.
'Dear, you never have it,
we deliver it.'
A judgement years proved true.
Certainly I've never had you
as you still have me, Caroline.

Why does a mother need a daughter?
Heart's needle, hostage to fortune,
freedom's end. Yet nothing's more perfect
than that bleating, razor-shaped cry
that delivers a mother to her baby.
The bloodcord snaps that held
their sphere together. The child,
tiny and alone, creates the mother.

A woman's life is her own
until it is taken away
by a first particular cry.
Then she is not alone
but part of the premises
of everything there is:
a time, a tribe, a war.
When we belong to the world
we become what we are.

Anne Stevenson

Birth

When they gave you to me you were redolent
Of acrid badly-made soap and blood,
And indeed you were covered with a waxy layer,
Like rice-paper on a macaroon, or cottage cheese.
You had obviously done some very heavy laundry
In the womb, using soda, wringing your hands,
Purple and sodden like a washer-woman,
Whose feeble fingers have mandarin's nails
With which you scratched your face, adding
To the general air of wear and tear and age,
And yet you were so young, a few minutes,
And the placenta not yet flowering in the bowl,
Your doll's clothes still airing, your air-way
Choked with mucus. All night we drained
You like a boiled potato, tipping you up
And, newly washed, we looked upon your great
High forehead, and your thin crop of hair,
And marvelled that you had travelled so far
Through such a small tunnel, no cuts,
No stitches, no forceps, just a long journey
And a small body, like a fish, sliding neatly
Into a quiet house, and an old bed,
Where no other child had been born before.
You cried a little, and then, exhausted, fell
Into the deepest sleep there is, apart
From death, and I lay flat and empty
Awake all night, tired beyond sleep,
Fearing and hoping beyond all bounds
That you would not live to curse your birth
As many have done before you,
And will do again.

Elizabeth Bartlett

Mother

Four times I was in that place. I leaned so far
into the hot centre of the wind, plunged belly-first
down into the dark birthing water
where howling creatures
push and clamour and cling.

Four times I was in that place, four times
torn, four times delivered
from my drowning.
That part was simple.
It was all that followed
that left me gasping for breath.

Jacqueline Saphra

The Wee Tin House Painted Pink

Acute admission, chest pain, aged 42
tubby, mis-shapen, looks 60
3 months pregnant, threatening miscarriage
last child 13 months, youngest of 20.
History includes, 2 still births
2 cot deaths, a spontaneous abortion.

A son brings the baby in to be breastfed
but his mother has arrested.
The boy and the baby are crying.
A cleaner bringing tea recognises
they're from the wee tin house painted pink
at the top of the old mountain road
with the lop-sided caravan alongside
and hedges draped with washing on fine days.

Kate MacDonell

Intensive Care

Golden girl under the blue light
small chest rising and falling.
I lift you out of your transparent crib;
you murmur, look at me with a puzzled frown.

I unbutton: you shake your head until
your furious gums lock on. My womb
convulses, remembering we were
two orchids wound upon the same stem.

I thought that like the boy you couldn't live,
felt again his clutching for breath;
but you persisted, held on tight,
tore at my flesh, demanded love.

Christine Bousfield

Poaching

You could assemble a whole catalogue of 'do's and don'ts' on the subject of poaching eggs . . .
Don't attempt to poach more than two unless you are a really experienced hand.
                    Delia Smith's Cookery Course, Part 1

She has heard the women whispering
in hospital rooms of suffering,
pain, blood.

She has stood palefaced in the margins
looking and listening, separate
from them.

While they slept, she has walked in her head
through the bluelit quiet ward, skirting
the nurse,

toe-stepped along the white corridor,
keeping to walls, to where milky kids
snuffle;

she's walked further to a flurried place
where infants lie flat under glass, taped
to tubes.

31

Sleepwalking, she has understood theft,
the urge to prise open, steal and hide,
not care

that another woman is crying somewhere
just so long as her own boat of arms
is full.

Jacqueline Brown

The Hammer Stone

Bury you deep my unlived child
bone of my bone. Bind you in ligaments
lock you in stone: no lynx or hyena
with claws like pain shall defile or dare
dig you up.

       Be safe in the dark
as you were in me. Shuttered and small
as the shrew or vole whose footsteps patter
like acorns falling on leaves.

I will lay you for comfort and warmth
on the wing of a swan
lay you down in the earth under the curve
of antler and horn.

       You will not know
the thrusting spear, the blood of killer and boar.
You will not know the kiss of a woman
heating a man like fire.

       You will not even know
me, my little lost son
or my heart like a hammer stone
heavy by you.

Mandy Pannett

Let-Down
for Medbh McGuckian

When my milk came in, oh not *my* milk, the child's –
well whose? can I say clearly? though I did
taste it once, a thin hazelnut water –
well, when it came in, it stood blue-veined in my breasts
and I could not express it. My breasts were as hard to grip
as Hallowe'en apples, the ones you hang on strings
from a clothes airer hauled to the ceiling, and try to bite.
Oh my breasts were hard as Bramleys
and my nipples tender as a cut.
The child could not catch on. How would she, the scrap?
And she wept, and the other babies around me wept
for the milk I had and to spare, but could not express.

When I no longer could lay my arms by my sides
and the midwife was threatening a drug to suppress lactation
it came to me, the dark shed in Rathmullen
and the child I was that summer, pressing all
the left side and the ear of her head against
the leathern flank of the cow, pulling, learning
the rhythm, the teat music
as the milk jet jangled onto galvanised metal
or drove richly into the foam of itself.
That double note. The sound of relief.
The nee-naw rhythm of rescue.

The child that was me couldn't, of course, get the hang.
But the mother I suddenly am hears the pitch of percussion
deepen as the bucket fills, its long diminuendo…
My shirt front's wringing, and when I unfasten my bra
two jets of milk rise in two crossing arcs
right over the head of my nuzzling wavery child.

Catherine Byron

33

Saving Dragons

Three in the morning and the house dark
except for the light from the lamp on the Aga.
The man and older child sleep
but she suckles the baby.

This is her time. The child's
warm body against her skin.
She chuckles the nape of his neck,
admires his lashes, so unnaturally long.

Through the glass of the kitchen door
she can see the garden, a black rectangle,
and the only sounds are the child's
suck, her own breath.

There's not a thought in her head
just the cream and satin of content.
She is milk and body. The child
slips from her teat, sleeps.

She settles him in the shawl,
imagines him tall and grand,
the adventures they'll have
saving dragons, killing maidens.

Patricia Bishop

from: Entries on Light

Staring up from his pram to the sky
   through mobile leaves that so
transfixed him, no matter who smiled
   and cooed, whose head might suddenly
block his light, those sea-washed eyes
   that had never yet seen sea
wouldn't flinch, barely blinked
   and when at last they panned from
tree to you, it would seem as if
   time itself had been scanned
so slowly did sight catch up with vision
   vision give way to a human hold.

And though he'd sit for hours, tearless
   and wide awake, you'd lift him
shoulder him with kisses, words, any
   bauble waved like a flag to bring it
home to him, him home to you.
   But even his eyelashes, so long
and straight, channelled his gaze
   outwards and onwards and irises
so light, so green, implied nothing
   but light behind them, as if his mind
had fled to the back of his skull
   and bled every shadowy lobe.

As you carried him in to a sunless
   hall, behind your back, were
those eyes trained down on a lane
   where the pram still stood?
A white sheet rumpled, an awning
   of leaves shadowed on sheet
and hood. As you shifted his weight
   and revolved to the door
between him and the light, did something
   pass – like a tryst, deferred
drawn up through those eyes to a sky
   he was saying goodbye to?

Mimi Khalvati

Thomas

By the simple act of leaning
from my arms, he makes me
disappear. And reappear at will,
and disappear again.

I watch his surprise,
an idea dawning, that chuckle.
Today he's a god,
where he goes I go too.

Later he'll bang a fist
on his reflection, eat his face
in a spoon and stand alone,
wondering who he is.

Carole Bromley

Didn't hurt

I remember the moment when
I gave up hitting my child.

She was two years old.
She was roaring wild.
It was midnight, toad cold.

If you don't shut up, I said,
I'll give you a smack.
She didn't. I did. Crack.

She wouldn't cry. There were no tears.
Instead she looked at me as if
I were her bitter foe. She said:
Didn't hurt.

So I hit her again, only harder.
Still no tears. Her eyes stretched wide.
Didn't hurt, she cried.

Her little voice, so small, so tough
stopped my raised hand. Enough.
I saw the future; endless blows,
endless defiance down the years.
The hitting and hating, hands and words.

It hurt. I wept.
I asked forgiveness, and she slept.

Ann Alexander

Zagharit

I ask them how they do it –
how they make it –
the *youyou* cry, *zagharit,*
memorable and elemental,
that could carry ships, lift a child,
celebrate a revolution.

The women are here
in beaded dresses and they dance
upstairs in a separate room,
they dress you, three years old,
in a white satin shirt
and a crimson waistcoat
with gold embroidery.

You are wearing white satin billowing
trousers and pointed slippers, gold
and crimson just like the waistcoat,
and a crimson and gold cap over your curls.
Your father, his cousins, our friends
are waiting downstairs
and you keep taking off the cap
and we keep putting it back on.

And when everything is ready –
the lace frill on your shirt –
we all stand at the top of the stairs
and the women begin to cry
that piercing, throbbing continuous cry
that is the transformation of pain,
or the creation of pain
to make room for joy,
and I take you by the hand
and the women follow you downstairs
into the bright company.

Jane Duran

Colouring In

She settles them to it
tucking their wriggling bodies
into red and blue overalls
compact as paint squares.
Her gaze holds down their shimmering heads
as she fiddles with her ring
lets her hand flutter over her stomach
pushes aside the newspaper
watching her children,
willing them.
As if every shaky outline
could be filled in with blocks of living colour
and the shape made whole.

Caroline Natzler

Head Lice

She stands by my bed in her nightie,
hair like Medusa
from scratching.
I bury the thought
with that flicker
of my mother's shuddering,
more at her memories
of cropped heads and paraffin
than at anything crawling on my scalp.

But then I see two flecks
crossing paths on her parting,
flitting under the canopy of hair,
as though I'm the one invading.

Her flinching from the fumes
feels like a hard pinch of blame,
but as I preen and pick,
meticulous as a monkey mother,
she is settled.

I catch five in a steel comb.
We watch their throes
on a piece of kitchen roll.
One speck drifts towards another.
She grabs my arm,
It's looking for its mother.

Karen Buckley

Picking Up Speed
(For Zoë)

She has discovered crop-tops.
Her favourite colour is pink.
A harem of Barbies circles the floor of her bedroom.

I'm a one man woman she hollers in the bath
glitter polish peeling from her nails.
In 'Beauty and the Beast' she doesn't like the prince.

Tonight she'll say *Sleep with me*
and you'll rub her skinny back
until breath snickers in her nose
then peel yourself
from her, picking up speed
as you cross the room. You daren't
look back.

Lynne Rees

Part-time Father

You pull away in the car,
not meeting my eyes, as the child stands,
gathering herself; and then

she comes to me, bright-faced,
her tight fist holding you secret;
ready to remember herself in my arms.

Jessica Penrose

Broken Moon

for Emma

Twelve, small as six,
strength, movement, hearing
all given in half measure,
my daughter,
child of genetic carelessness,
walks uphill, always.

I watch her morning face;
precocious patience as she hooks each sock,
creeps it up her foot,
aims her jersey like a quoit.
My fingers twitch;
her private frown deters.

Her jokes can sting:
'My life is like dressed crab
– lot of effort, rather little meat.'
Yet she delights in seedlings taking root,
finding a fossil,
a surprise dessert.

Chopin will not yield to her stiff touch;
I hear her cursing.
She paces Bach exactly,
firm rounding of perfect cadences.
Somewhere inside
she is dancing a courante.

In dreams she skims the sand,
curls toes into the ooze of pools,
leaps on to stanchions.
Awake, her cousins take her hands;
they lean into the waves,
stick-child between curved sturdiness.

She turns away from stares,
laughs at the boy who asks
if she will find a midget husband.
Ten years ago, cradling her,
I showed her the slice of silver in the sky.
'Moon broken', she said.

Carole Satyamurti

Growing Up

My daughter poses in front of the mirror
with nothing on. She leans, arms stretched
above her head, trying on faces, and I wake
from months of blindness; this preening girl
has wintered in the darkness of her clothes
the curve of hips, the swell of breasts.
She's pouting now, lips in league
with her sultry gaze. She sways, provocative
as a lap dancer, her feet missing
the plastic figures she was playing with
just half an hour before.

Dorothy Baird

Boy, Part 1

He has eyes like stone, my son,
a blank grey gaze that chills.
What is it that has snuffed out
childhood? I don't know where he is.
How can I say I don't, that
I can't even talk to him? They say
'You've got to show who's boss,
Mrs Hills,' as if it's simple.
They don't know he's shut the door.
Some days I shout as if I could
batter a way through to him,
or I try to think of things
to make him laugh. He's a kid,
after all. He's closed up tight.
One tea time I got in later
I heard him talking, like before.
He was with the little ones,
playing. When he saw me his eyes
changed. Blank. I am afraid for him.

Cynthia Fuller

Joy

It's June, it's hot, it's raining
and you've shorn off
nearly all your hair
dyed the rest black
and you're my child.
We've been at this bus stop
for over half an hour,
cars surfing past, stirring a brew
from blocked gutters
to chuck up at our feet

and yet the air's still sweet
as apricots, the Late-Nite shop
is open, and your father's girl
has given you a leather jacket
once owned, so she says,
by Tony Curtis's wife,
and even though you're fifteen,
and I don't for one moment
imagine you'll have noticed,
you are holding my hand.

Alex Josephy

Graffiti

Stumbling for a switch, tying a knot
in my Parisian dressing gown, I know
what I'm going to find

three o'clock in the morning. I'm unbolting
the front door with excuses.
They'll be different from yesterday's

and in the porch-light two policemen
are holding you from a night
I don't seem able to.

One is kind, adopts
an absent-father role, pep talks
about the dangers out there.

The other lectures me on child protection
but I'm not listening. I'm travelling
down the Jubilee Line, glueing back

your world, while your window
still hangs open, highlighting your escape
and rain pours in.

Wendy French

5

Willendorf Venus

My man showed me the stone he'd carved,
said it was me. It had my curls
but was not like the women I know.

I have big breasts, fed my ten children,
but these boobs were enormous,
also the hips and stomach
and the labia,
curved as my lips.

If I could carve a stone I'd make a man.
He would be tall and strong
just like my man.

I'd give him hands and arms for bow and arrows
to kill the wild black boar and the red deer,
and make him a big penis, long as his arms,
to give me ten more children.

Alice Beer

The Willendorf Venus: *an archaeological find in a remote valley in the Austrian Alps, 4 inches high, estimated about 25,000 years old.*

Working Out

I hate those women who work out
 – their muscled, sanctimonious bums –
why must they always jog about
and boast of weight-loss to their chums?

I watch them as they swoop and rush
to thwack the ball round tennis courts
and bet they've all got raging thrush
inside their skintight lycra shorts.

I hate the way they go for runs –
why don't they stop to lean on gates,
dance blues to sky-larks, guzzle buns,
write sonnets, eat off cardboard plates?

44

I wish they'd read and laze and dream,
pick asphodel and bubble ballads –
instead of which they give up cream
and toy with cautious tuna salads.

If they would only binge on chips
 – while scribbling plots of love or gore –
they might get bigger round the hips
but oh – I'd like them so much more!

Mary Sheepshanks

Remedial Action

It took her weeks, months,
to make the appointment
but when at last she saw him
and asked if he could, perhaps,
do something, anything,
about her breasts,
he nodded and cupped them
in his hands so tenderly
that her eyes filled with tears
and, half in love with him,
she listened as he warned her
that surgery had its dangers,
and might in this case
cause her to lose
sensation in the nipples,
which made her yearn to tell him
that nipple-sensation was,
like orgasm, a gift she'd never had
though often longed for
but then she remembered –
how once, just once, suckling
her last child, she had felt,
hadn't she? a sweet, slow pull,
an ecstatic tugging that seemed
to run from breast to womb.

Angela Kirby

On Turning Forty

and losing my dash and my flim-flam,
on shedding my snake-skin of glamour,
my lustre, my pollen, the dew on my finish,
the dust on my three-quarter profile
in sunlight. This is to record
my old fluff and feathers, my snoods
and my boas, my velvets crushed
smooth as suede and imbedded with sweat
and a perfume called 'Wrappings'
which you can't buy any more,

and to say I'm just sorry I didn't
own more. I wish I'd had closets
of silks hooked like game birds, racks
of sandals and slippers and strappy
stilettos stretched out on their shoetrees
like leopards in heat. I wish I'd had
powder exploding from winter-fox puffs
and bottles with knitted silk bulbs,
and pearls, and a silver-backed hairbrush,
and a triplicate candlelit looking-glass altar

so I could have sat down and met her,
that terrific tall creature who stalked me
in restaurants, shadowed me on streets
of dark plate-glass windows, squared up
to me suddenly in toilets in bars. Because
now she is gone, I think forever,
and this pleasant-faced person here
smiling instead. I want to say I am sorry
I turned from her embarrassed, never
reached out my hands, led her out on the floor.

Kate Clanchy

Women Who Dye Their Hair

Some of us have done it since our twenties
when our hair turned white on the death of a loved one
or it ran in the family like baldness, and some of us
spray red or purple on shaved stubble,
and others have let it creep up on us,
counting the odd hair, then the fifth, the fiftieth,
till our teenagers point out how old we're getting
but our lovers who hate anything artificial
like makeup and sequins, though they accept
icecream and the Pill, say we shouldn't bother,
so we steal home from Boots with the ColorGlo
and lock ourselves in the bathroom in rubber gloves,
emerge an hour later ten years younger
with a smart grey streak over one temple
and mahogany smudges round the jaw line.
And when the roots start to show we carelessly
pop into the hairdresser and book a colour
which means a cut and blow and takes all morning
so we can catch up on our reading, extending
our knowledge of the stars and multiple orgasm,
but we have to go every six weeks or it starts to fade
and by now the local firm is turning our hair to hay
so we find a better one at forty quid a splash,
a rollercoaster we can't get off of,
and we decide to let it all grow out and be our age
which isn't a hundred and five but might as well be.

Janet Fisher

The Thieves

A period, you'd imagine, is no use
to anyone, but the woman who owns it,
who thought she held it secure

in the safe of her body.
Yet thieves broke in and grabbed it,
took it instead of her jewellery:

She's forty-nine, she won't miss it –
we'll just take one, maybe two.
On the other hand, we'll have the lot,

47

stash them away. Nothing to boast about.
Not anything you'd forget, though.
To make off with them on a quiet night –

it's like stealing the darkness itself,
or taking the moon, bowling it away,
expecting it to retain its glow.

Moniza Alvi

Screen Test

I strip to the waist
in the breast scanning caravan's cubicle:
an aging Page Three Girl shape,
my bosom milky pink,
blue veined and crêpey
with soft, pale nipples.

The kind, brisk radiologist instructs me
to contort myself in Picasso posture,
elbows raised asymmetrically.
I rest the right half of my 38DD
on the glass X-ray table under spotlights,
try to scoop my left boob out of shot,
hand overflowing.

The angle-poised plate firmly squishes
my right breast down
like a ripe peach –
a Damien Hurst sort of sandwich
which might vie for the Turner Prize.

A leaflet stresses the importance
of buying a bra which fits you.
Chance would be a fine thing!
No such model exists for me
even at Rigby and Peller of Knightsbridge,
the Queen's corsetières.

My back aches and bends
after decades of bad engineering.
As a teenager and young woman
I was perplexed at men smirking appreciatively
when I said I lived in Bristol.

If only Isambard Kingdom Brunel
could have applied his genius
to designing a suspension bridge
for my bristols,
as Howard Hughes did for Jane Russell,
though she outlawed it.

Philippa Lawrence

Scan

Together we explore my inner landscape on the screen.
He plots a course and charts me frame by frame.
See, here's your pancreas, your spleen, he chats,
and over here, this, the outline of your liver.

I watch my abdomen appear in monochrome.
Ghost-shapes float haloed, flickering like neon-signs.
I expect Apollo to land, a space-suited man step out,
glide strangely slowly across my contours with a flag.

The radiologist has moved his cursor, clicked.
The image on the monitor splits in two.
One half zooms in, zooms in again
to where circles bright as Saturn's rings

cast hard-edged shadows stretching in between.
Mare Frigoris, Mare Nubrium, Sea of Cold,
Sea of Clouds. *Lacus Aestruum, Oceanus Procellarum*,
Seething Lake and Ocean of Storms.

I kneel behind a crater full of stars
as data ricochets across the void. The spaceman
plants his flag in the spot marked X, leaves moonboot tracks
like 'cut here' lines along my ovarian tract.

That night I'm in the orchard among the apple trees.
The hens have shaken out their duvets in the roots.
I slide my hand under a warmth of breast, find
a perfect egg to hold against the black. Obliterate the moon.

Pat Borthwick

Still Life With Figs

An untidy package, all its granular guts
stuffed into a sort of beanbag. Skin
contains the seeds, holds them bottom-heavy
bellying to a slight sideways droop
from offcentre nipples. Faint vertical veins
do not succeed in corseting their shape,
their generous opulence. And the colour!
— they are plush, dull purple. Washed,
a faint grey bloom vanishes, returns with dryness.
I get a knife, halve one, am shocked
by brightness — scarlet seeds in scarlet flesh,
and the rind between them and the skin
(that smoky plum-colour) is a wholly surprising
pale greenish cream, the sort of colour
that looks smooth to the touch. It is.
But a quartered fig has nothing to hold its shape,
no inner membrane, no tension
nipple to base. That point of skin,
released, lifts, and the tiny seeds begin to fall,
a few at a time, bright on the white plate.
And suddenly I'm thinking
of my own sliced skin, my own severed
breast, fallen away into a dish.

Joanna Boulter

Amazon
for Grevel

For four months
all those Matisse and Picasso women
draped against
plants, balconies, Mediterranean sea, skies
have taunted me
with the beautiful globes of their breasts as I've filled

my emptiness
with pages of scrawl, with fecund May, its floods
of green, its irrepressible
wedding-lace white, buttercup gold,
but failed to cover
the image of myself as a misshapen clown

until you reminded me
that in Greek myth the most revered women
were the single-breasted
Amazons who mastered javelins and bows, rode
horses into battle,
whose fierce queens were renowned for their femininity.

Then recognising the fields I'd fought my way across
I raised my shield
of glistening words, saw it echoed the sun.

Myra Schneider

Knocking On

Past fifty, past that five-barred gate
    I shall not climb again,
my dazzled eyes appreciate
    the beauty of young men.

When I was in my upper teens
    and looked in young men's eyes
I saw, reflected in each lens,
    my beauty shrunk in size

but full of power. I sensed the awe
    that fed my vanity
but when I too felt their desire
    my power drained from me.

Past seventy, I still revere
    the beauty of the young
but know that it must disappear
    like mine, before too long,

into a crumpled parchment bag
    with hair turned grey, or white;
and sight of pantaloon, or hag,
    kills Eros dead with fright.

So we are left with Agapé –
    let all the mirrors shiver –
look outward, active empathy
    translates the sensual fever:

but sometimes, still, the young men leap
    across dream's five-barred gate
and Eros frolics through my sleep –
    so late in life, so late!

Anna Adams

Disturbing Ripples

She's almost forgotten this part
It hardly troubles her now
Sometimes her soapy hand
In the bath wakens a whisper
Accidentally

And she wonders what
A spot of auto-erotic fun
Would do to her emotional stability.

The bath water cools and the book
Waiting in the fireside chair
Lures her away from dangerous
Shoals and eddies

But combing her hair
And putting on clean white
Tedious underwear
Sighing quietly she remembers
Glorious trumpet blasts
And raucous laughter when you press
A mouth against a navel
And blow.

Elizabeth Birchall

Vanity

My poor old breasts
soft and flat and sunken

as two ineptly-cooked
Yorkshire puddings,

empty old breasts
well-read but floppy,

as lax and loose
as gone-elastic

left in a sad drawer,
sulky pair,

six months older
than the breasts

of the mistress
of the Prince of Wales,

shifty customers:
but you kiss them,

you say – no, not so,
as peachy and girl-firm

as ever...
You liar,

kissing old breasts
that can still blush

into mothiness.

Penelope Shuttle

6

Coming of Age

Like boys at the first windfall
of conkers, spiders at the first frisson
of autumn, this June day's midsummer
sunshine has brought you out: old women

risking pastels, blatantly bare-legged –
you whose grandson years ago stuck up
my daughter's hair with playdoh,
you, who used to drive me round

for Meals on Wheels and knew each
name but always called me 'Florence' –
in shorts even. How you brazen out
aging, exposing varicose wirings,

melting ankles, bird-legs; how you dress up
your crowning glory's lack-lustre
with wild hats or dyeing or just waving.
Straight-backed, defiantly driving

or blocking access with zimmers,
shopping trolleys, inexorable as tanks
you get your own back on skateboarders,
those youths who at night darken your doorways.

I'm not one of you yet, but as I wait behind
you in queues, you already acknowledge me
differently, recognise markings, the backs
of my hands, how I stand against sunlight.

And I catch your private humming, pick up
a sweetish brittle scent of something folded
inward; half glimpse beyond smudged lipstick,
runnels of eye-shadow, your small fierce glances,

your reedy intimacies, your painful optimism,
things I've also known and dreamed of, never told.
A kind of pollen count. O bright, brave,
indomitable old women, I'm coming, I'm coming.

Frances Wilson

Who Are You?

I wonder what he sees,
am almost unnerved.
Aged five months
he scrutinises me
with puzzled inquiry.

Bold hazel eyes
brighter than blackbird's
slowly take me in.

'It's Granny!' I pipe.
'It's your Granny!'

Suddenly sun bursts
out past cloud,
he smiles
and I know I am.

Dinah Livingstone

What do you do all day while I'm at school?
For Leah, my grand daughter

Did you expect me to list
the potatoes in need of peeling,
what fish I choose for lunch
or how many times I dust the rooms?

No, no, awake or asleep
I dream, my love,
as most of us do.
Dream of golden horses in fields of cowslips,
peace in a land always beautiful
no wars, violence or hurt.

Like you, I withdraw from the world of reality
my hands grope for the path at night
my feet tread carefully to avoid lines.
Spaces fill with crotchets, quavers
a melody to rise
over dizzy mountain slopes
where prayer-wheels whirl and clatter
and rhododendrons riot.

Anne Beresford

Ambushed by notes
for my mother

Ambushed by notes,
those little notes he sends you,

your eldest grandson,
in the bottom of the sugar pot –

'white sugar is very bad for our bodies',
and on your shopping list –

'get organic',
and a daughter's message

telling you to put a little oil
in the bath water,

or the carer's, reminding you
what's there for lunch.

They skip the target,
they are vanishing faces,

the absent faces of care,
and your mind brushes past them

like knee-high wet grass
in the early morning.

Sue MacIntyre

Heartsease

A warm night after rain, I step outside
and smell the new-washed air that emanates
from roses in the gardens of the town
and from the bedrooms where the young girls lie
wakeful in tented sheets, their hearts aflame
for lovers in their still undreamt-of dreams.
Another shower sends me back indoors
to my own garden mirrored in the rain;
I close my window in a sudden chill
and drink my cocoa in a spindrift shawl.

Morning again, and pansies barely dry
are little battered flags of brilliance
growing in cracks between my paving stones.
Heartsease, you called them, and for love of you
I touch their petals with a gentle hand
and pick the weathered dead-heads carefully.

My garden is a meadow lush with weeds
in whose green depths such hidden flowers grow
as one day will suffice for all your needs.
I thought so once, sadly uncertain now
I cherish flowers that thrived on my neglect
and throw the weeds upon the rising heap.
Yet, in my seventieth year, I am ashamed
because of all the things I have not done,
the sins committed in my carelessness;
you told me once my greatest talent was
simply for loving, now I need to know
that heartsease pansies still have power to heal.

Elizabeth Bewick

Confabulation

Curled in her wheelchair she addresses the lounge;
Somebody help me. You. Come here at once!
I have money. I can pay. Nobody answers.
There is a hunching of shoulders, eyes shift to the floor.
In the silence her anger grows.
How fat and ugly you are and, what is more,
you all stink. I can smell you from here, unwashed,
your dinners dried round your lips. Getting into her stride
she never uses the f-word or invokes God.

She turns to me; *It is nauseating to watch you*
fawn over that man, holding his hand,
spooning his food. Why don't you help me scrub
the kitchen floor! He'll be alright. Her face is worn
but, under the lizard skin, etched bones are memorable;
her eyes still wide and blue as a child's.
She watches me closely, sees my silent tears,
then quietly says: *You adore him, don't you?*
And we gaze at each other, speechless.

Margaret Perry

Dementia

My mother crosses my path.
The winter birches hide and don't hide her
and there is a sense at moments
of a visual lapse, a complicity

as she falls back inevitably
and forgets to finish her sentences,
her scattered thinking. When we talk
there is a forest in her imagination
and one in mine. If we combine them,
the sparse trees she remembers

and those I imagine make up a dense wood
where both of us are reassured and sheltered.
Beyond that we have an understanding
I know how to calm her – how to turn
these inconsistencies around, fill in the spaces
abandoned now by her memory,
so the day shines and she is still in it.

Jane Duran

Lost

Stone-age, stone-grey eyes
clear in her glove-like skin;
a look of having been ironed
before she shuffled in.

Cradling a pink blonde doll
in a quilted bag, pink satin,
she lifts it out a while,
she puts it back again.

Her dead child? Poor, poor lady.
We burn to know...*what reason?*
No sign, from mouth or body.
She stuns our pity, even.

Anne Stevenson

Mushrooms

Have you found them, before day glowers,
Their nestled domes in glistening white
From heavy dews which whispered light
Simpler than kisses? They are earth's true flowers.

Their scent is ground's breath, older than the sun,
Frills pinker than a child's nail
Not rank brown ribs laid out for sale.
Snap the stalks quickly, for the small worms come.

How many live by fields now? Of her
This rises suddenly, the cull
My father made, a lunchbox full.
I smelt black perfume drifting up the stairs,

His autumn supper, called, awake too late,
"Mushrooms – ?" sank, slept, awoke to find
Her, so rarely lit and quiet, her hands
Fine earth, the mushrooms steaming on the plate.

Alison Brackenbury

Secret

These women have it.
They are holding something secret,
something special; this one is in her bed,
her room, with all the women round her.
All the women tending her.
Her make up is put on; the finest touch;
two take the plum silk sari
and between them, perfect equals, guide
its softly slipping rustle overhead.
Precious stones come lovingly from box to bed
to skin. All the women hold her hands.
A barrel seeps the smell of roses,
where a girl is kneeling, lifting petals,
sifting them through fingertips like flour,
while here, the youngest one is making
brush strokes, like the ones she used
when grandma came from bathing; soft,
washed smooth and settling; before;
before the strange new smell of death
in this, her hair.

Cathy Grindrod

Part 2

Portraits

Essential Equipment

The steel stays that pushed through frayed seams from
her grubby corsets – their strange lingerie colours:
soap-greyed white, watery sepia black or
the livid faded mauve of fading cabbage roses,
and the desert tones: henna, ochre, terra-
cotta, of ointment stains, cosmetic smears
on greasy crumpled tissues and wads of cotton
that blurred her dressing-table's glassy surface;

the enema bag on the back of the bathroom door
its ridged rubber tube and metal clip,
the raw red bulb of her douche syringe and
her shiny leather bunion shield, the tweezers,
scissors, curling tongs like torture instruments;
all those tools and objects – appurtenances
of the female – were the burdens she assumed,
the gear she used: her essential equipment.

Ruth Fainlight

Annie Taylor, 24 October 1901

It's often been voiced that fools rush in
where angels fear to tread,
so when Annie Taylor went over the Falls
that's exactly what was said.

We're talking turn of the century,
we're talking long-skirted dames,
we're talking unheard of courage,
we're talking forgotten names.

Yet it wasn't a fool or an angel
who made this appalling descent,
just a woman who needed the money
for the bills for the food and the rent.

They padded her into a barrel,
pumped air in and screwed down the lid,
called good-bye, good luck and God speed
as into the river it slid.

First it bounced around in the rapids
then moved to the edge with a rush,
fell down through the mist and into the foam
to the gasps of the crowd in the crush.

She emerged a bit dazed but alive,
felt the fame and the fortune that day,
First Person to Conquer the Falls,
signed photos and made people pay.

For a further twenty-one years
The Queen of the Mist worked on,
standing next to an old wooden barrel,
all the fame and the money long gone.

Karin Koller

Unrecorded Speech (1)

She says 'How was you?' Kissing. 'Come on in,
I'm all of a muck-sweat, having a merry-go-round;
you've caught me doing my work.'
She doesn't clean, but circumvents the dirt.
Chairs stand on tables – 'All of a tizz-wozz'.
(Has that been spelt before?) 'A lick of paint',
she says, propping her brush in turps,
'freshens things up a bit'. She paints the door
and skirting boards; washes white window-veils.
Houses, bedsitters, flats, extend herself.
She makes the best of it but likes a move;
it's like a change of dress, changing address.
I've lost count of the changes. 'Home at last!'
was said too often to be credible.
We'll write it on her tomb, or jar of ash,
unless she sees us out.
She says 'The poor old lady' of someone
no older than herself.
'She's gone a bit – you know dear – gone a bit,
doo-lally. Poor old thing. It takes all sorts – '
From childhood she remembers sparkling frost,
and walking out in it in Christmas clothes –
a coat her mother made her – vivid mauve –
'so bright against the snow'.
'And of a Friday afternoon
the teacher read to us. That was the best.'
Stories have been essential food since then.
Peg's Paper, H. E. Bates, Hardy and all
except romances; 'that don't interest me.'
She fills her days 'somehow', since Hubby died,
but she has grown since then.
'All in a lifetime, dear,' she says of death.
Her words may be dead language soon;
that's why I write them down. They will be heard
'never no more', as she said at the birth
of my husband, her only child,
proving that double negatives mean 'No'.

Anna Adams

90th Birthday

Awa wi ye! ye're hae'in me oan!
Thon wifie ower there's nae ninety.
Jist leuk at her, sittin 'ere buskit and bonny
weel riggit oot in new claes,
douce an canty wi shinin grey een
an skin like a teen age quine;
neen o yer funcy lotions an muck,
soap an rain waater wis aa that hers got.

She his the strinth o twa muckle Clydsedales,
niver shirkit a lang day's darg,
disna tak til her bed wi a snocherty cald
bit warsles on throu't wi a lach.

She kens aa aboot aabody
keeps up with the clash
keps her bairns in order
settles their hash;
fin she maks em their supper
it's oot ti the yaird wi a graip in her han
ti dig up a bilin of tatties.

There's great-great grand bairns rinnin
in til the hoose with cairdies, han vrocht
picters an news – fa did fit, fan an faar,
foo an fit wye – fit stories an sic ongyangs!
But kindly ullfashence, a bosie a piece
clarted wi her ane hame made jam,
they ken the warld's a richt gweed place
wi a grunny aye there an at han.

Mary Johnston

Babcia Zosia

Oj Babciu
I never got a chance to tell you.
No bo niby jak, kiedy?
I loved your gravelly voice
even lower than Babcia Kicia's
and everyone thought she was a bloke.

"Eye um nott sur, Eye um madam!"
she'd bellow down the phone.
You rasped like a jazz singer
in some smokey dive bar,
gruff with sex.

Your voice didn't match how you looked
cropped, silver hair and sensible shoes.
Later I heard stories about you,
widowed young, no kids, driving
ambulances in the war, *oj Babciu.*

Za malo, za malo o Tobie wiem.
Your clothes were shabbier than ours.
We had our first electric fridge,
you put food out in snowdrifts on the sill.
We watched Dr.Who, while you tried

to get the BBC World Service on your radio,
when the Russians didn't jam the signal.
You promised you'd be back to see me,
 but you didn't sound sure,
'if I can save enough pennies', you said.
Oj Babciu. I already knew.

Maria Jastrzebska

Babcia – gran, granny

66

Nancy

That woman reared a tribe of pagans, my mother said,
and your father among them, knowing no better.
Until he married, of course, and shaking off his wicked mother
mended his ways and took to milk and Mass like water.
But we liked her, admired the corrugated hair,
the pearl drop earrings, her finger-nails a set of tiny pillar-boxes,
the sauntering high-heeled slippers where others trudged
in turbaned curlers, grey men's socks. And the language,
her neat painted mouth pulled down, regretful, prim,

And so I had to tell him straight, she'd say. *I told him
he could arseholes, for me.* Her final word on everything
from parsons down to royalty. Too bold by half, braving
the pit-top to tell the manager what he could do with his five bob,
refusing to stand for the Anthem in the Legion and barred *sine die*
for her favourite verb. *They can arseholes,* she'd shouted,
parasites, battening on the poor. As if the poor
were someone else, not here, not her with her debts
and her old scandals. (One Christmas Eve, she'd set off

for the butcher's and turned up next day with the goose,
legless, a disgrace. *I met some pals,* she told us,
You know how it is.) And how is it with thirteen kids
and weeks of strikes and a man who laughed and cried,
that pleased to see you back. How do you keep that fine hand fine;
the ring to the pawn, and in between – Monday to pay-day
it's cold water, black-lead, soda, and a sacking apron to wipe it on.
We knew nothing beyond your jokes, the birthdays, weddings,

parties lasting a week, you leading congas in the street,
your spindle legs tireless in the glassy shoes through your seventies,
your eighties. And then your daughters in their best colours,
clashing perfumes, the front room spiky with wreaths,
your quiet sons weeding out the lilies. *I'll not have lilies
in my house,* you'd said. *They're for the dead.
Any bugger dares to send me lilies. You know.
You can tell them what to do.*

Ann Sansom

67

Idaho Women

"Sing something ugly, Patty, till I get back."
Dottie strides out of the bar
her rump in narrow Wranglers.

Tiny behind the grand piano
Patty plays Mr. Bojangles
but it doesn't turn out ugly,
her voice husky in the mike.

Patty's all done up tonight –
jet earrings, sequinned dress,
bare shoulders. Her bones
are fine, like a sleek doe's.

Heads of pronghorns,
elk, deer hang on the walls,
trophies of men who hunt –
she sings to their glassy eyes.

Klaus the real estate man,
his belly stuffed in a rugby shirt,
sends Patty a cognac. She leaves it
beside the snifter of ones and fives.

She could be in Vegas
but she'd never leave the mountains –
with money from these gigs
she built herself a house
up Warm Springs Road,
all wood inside with high ceilings.

On her break she eases past
Klaus's gold-nugget hands,
orders a beer with Dottie. They hug
and chuckle like sharp-tailed grouse
about her new linens from J.C. Penney's,
her bedroom a splash of yellow eyelet
cotton: "You'll love it, Dottie."

Nancy Mattson

The Wife of Bafa

My name is Mrs Alice Ebi Bafa
I come from Nigeria.
I am very fine, isn't it.
My next birthday I'll be twenty-nine.
I'm business woman.
Would you like to buy some cloth?
I have all the latest styles from Lagos,
Italian shoe and handbag to match,
lace, linen and Dutch wax.
I only buy the best
and I travel first class.
    Some say I have blood on my hands
'cause I like to paint my nails red
but others call me femme fatale.
My father had four wives
so I've had five husbands.
I cast a spell with my gap-toothed smile
and my bottom power.
Three were good and two were bad.
    The first three were old and rich
and I was young and fit.
They died of exhaustion.
The fourth one was ladies' man.
I could not count his women on one hand
but he'd rage if I looked at another man.
I was very wild when I was young.
They called me Miss Highlife,
I was not considered a good wife
but I always respected my husband.
He died when I returned from this London.
    The last one I married for love.
He was studying law at University of Ibadon.
He was not yet twenty-one,
wicked in bed and so handsome
but he liked pornographic magazine.
His favourite was *Playboy*.
One day I threw it on fire
to teach him a lesson.
He turned into wife batterer.
He was to regret his action.
I beat him till he screamed for his ancestors.
Now we get on like a house on fire.
    Some say I'm a witchcraft
'cause I did not bear them children.
They do not understand your Western medicine.
    You like my headtie.

It's the latest fashion.
They sell like hot cake on Victoria Island.
Fifty pounds.
I give you discount 'cause I like your smile.
The quality is very good.
If I take off more I will not make profit.
I travel to Lagos next week.
Make it my lucky day.
Please, I beg you.

Patience Agbabi

The Ethics of Erotica

She's remarkably relaxed
for someone who sells
clitoris creams –

there's no hint
of a wince as she talks
about dildo volumes –

she counts the crotchless panties
in the same way she'd count
oven gloves

and gives women
who ask for dirty photos
a very clean look.

Zeeba Ansari

Sheela-na-gig

She's shrunken and tired, very tired:
more long-lived than Methuselah,
has seen it all before: war, rape, famine.

Cross-eyed, leering. No breasts, nipples.
Imp-like body. Fingers gripping open
the Mother-of-all birth-canals,

she's lost count of punters, damp afternoons.
One more grinning crew returning
to Birmingham, Newport, wherever.

She and her bestiary confront
long after all the pointing tourists
are gone, and though some giggle,

and some like schoolboys make cunt jokes,
the last laugh's with her. She'll be there
at the Judgement: with the monsters,

serpents swallowing their own tails,
the basilisk; the ram, the tyrant,
the little musician, the lovers;

to haul us back whole – repentant
or no – into that slack vulva.
She stares as you walk between black

yews towards your car; as you close
the gate to her ancient, egg-shaped
churchyard; consult a watch, road-map.

Sally Carr

Women Laughing

Gurgles, genderless,
Inside the incurious womb.

Random soliloquies of babies
Tickled by everything.

Undomesticated shrieks
Of small girls. Mother prophesies
You'll be crying in a minute.

Adolescents wearing giggles
Like chain-mail, against embarrassment,
Giggles formal in shape as
Butterpats, or dropped stitches.

Young women anxious to please,
Laughing eagerly before the punchline
(Being too naïve to know which it is).

Wives gleaming sleekly in public at
Husbandly jokes, masking
All trace of old acquaintance.

Mums obliging with rhetorical
Guffaws at the children's riddles
That bored their parents.

Old women, unmanned, free
Of children, embarrassment, desire to please,
Hooting grossly, without explanation.

U A Fanthorpe

Mothers Running

They ran at the news of a death
a death by drowning.
We clustered in gymslipped formality
at the window and watched them run;
head-scarved, overalled, shopping-bagged,
over roads, over fields, over boundaries forbidden to me,
the mothers came running.

They bore an unspoken question on their lips
and all would ask it.
We heard whispers down the corridor,
'The teacher jumped in.' 'Could do nothing.'
Oblivious of proper entrances,
they surged with adult audacity
across the invisible line dividing the boys' school
from our own:
over roads, over fields, over boundaries forbidden to me,
the mothers came running.

Now on a modern screen
a new school tragedy unfolds;
memory rolls back,
monochrome, sinister,
as the mothers come
running

Thelma Laycock

Mothers

"No. Go away!" I screamed at my mother
as she entered my dream in late adolescence,
shadow hanging over me like the past or the future.

In my book mothers were the tough ones,
sensible, feet flat on the ground, earth
bound to the realms of the possible.

Mothers were moody: their monthly cycle
like regular verses that opened expansively
with ice-cream after school, treats, new clothes
but whose lines shortened at the end of the month
as tempers and housekeeping money dwindled.

Mothers were clever but didn't show it,
deferred to children's and husband's brilliance;
the ancient history of the books they'd read
concealed except for the occasional gloss,
the dazzling and sometimes deflating footnote.

Mothers changed their names to Martha:
in the book I read their hands were busy,
their words grew bitter, burned the tongue.

Mothers were durable, almost unbreakable;
crushed by a cow against the wall
got up, carried on, so the story goes
a little more slowly, swallowing Veganin,
and watching the secret bruises yellow.

Kathleen McPhilemy

Thinking of you...

*On the 9.30 from Paddington
May 2002*

They joined the train at Didcot. Angel faces
On a school trip for pre-pubescent teens.
Bejewelled belly-buttons, dental braces;
All shrunken tops and elephantine jeans.
Now up and down the central aisle strides *Sir*
Seeing his jailbait cargo safely through;
He moves his lips as if in silent prayer,
Counts little titties and divides by two.
Mouthbreathing Tara's adenoidal whine,
Begging to borrow someone's mobile phone,
Descants a giggle-fugue in triple-time
And then it's Bristol Parkway, and they've gone.
If you were here, I'd catch your eye and say –
This Whitsun, I was late getting away...

Ann Drysdale

44 girls at a bus stop

The schoolgirls at the bus stop
swarm and clatter,
surge, break and splatter
like sea around a rock.
They have found the secret
of perpetual motion. One says
worms drop from the tree
that leans over the pavement.
'There ...', she screams,
sets off a stampede into the shelter,
crammed now, books and bags
slammed against chests and legs.

They wear black but look like rainbows,
catching all the light there is,
reflecting it back, bright with noise,
as they dash words back and forth.

Sophie Richmond

Piccadilly Line

Girls, dressed for dancing,
board the tube at Earl's Court,
flutter, settle.
Chattering, excited by a vision
of glitter, their fragile bodies
carry invisible antennae,
missing nothing.
Faces velvet with bright camouflage,
they're unsung stars – so young
it's thrilling just to be away from home.

One shrieks, points, springs away.
She's seen a moth
caught up in the blonde strands
of her companion's hair,
a moth marked
with all the shadow colours of blonde.
The friend's not scared;
gently she shakes her head,
tumbles it, dead,
into her hands.

At Piccadilly Circus they take flight,
skim the escalator,
brush past the collector,
up to the lure of light.

Carole Satyamurti

Part 3

Work

For the Shetland Lace-knitters

Time clings to a wisp of light:
spindrift, hairstreak, salt-spray.
The spindle lisps, the treadle rocks.

Soft as starlight or a dunter's down,
how the stole floats round your shoulders,
wool become wing, moorland made air,

as white as a tammie norie's breast,
as rock-cress clinging to the Keen.
Listen: you can hear the moon singing.

Enter the pattern, diamonds in diamonds,
chamfered waves. Watch them fall
round Humla Stack, the Holm of Skaw.

Love leads the weave, the lilting hours,
a woman sitting, haar at her door,
the dark at her back, mist in her fingers.

Stitch by stitch: a flick of her thumb.
Loop by loop the white poems come.

Lynne Wycherley

dunter – eider
Keen – Keen of Hamar
tammie norie – puffin

77

1

A Visit to the Museum

My people made nails like these,
beaten sharp, cut from the rod.
The museum grate is filled with paper
but some sense of toil touches us:
the tiny window, the rotten door.

In a nailhouse like this, six by four,
Greatgrandmama kept her children fed.
Being widowed she had little choice,
and her mother, widowed too and aged, had less.
So they sweated together, sang their hymns.
In Summer they would have stripped to the waist.
The children's play was sweeping and packing,
blowing bellows. Bellows like these.

Pauline Kirk

For Bread – 1920s

Not lust but hunger made them use this ploy
To live together as a family:
Two children, man and wife. Her heavy body
Adequate as male in tweeds and boots, ready

For labouring. They wanted bread, and bread
Meant work. The queue of unemployed was curling
Round the block. She stood there cold and waiting
With the other men. Her husband dead.

A factory was wanting a strong man
And took her on as a handy caretaker.
Also as nightwatchman. But then a fire
Flared and she was wounded by a falling stone,

Was rushed to hospital covered in blood.
The wife and children silent by her bed
To fear and hear their fable-world collapse
When sneering nurses named her secret sex.

Lotte Kramer

Grandma makes a Spitfire – Grandma wins the war

Standing in the door, dark-haired, slender,
leaning lazily against the frame,
she smokes a gasper, laughing lewdly,
head tipped back, beret at a stylish angle.

From the floor I see her elongated,
stretched to the ceiling in dungarees.
She stoops to stroke my baby cheek,
kiss me with tobacco scented mouth.

She paints her lips with scarlet, like her scarf,
and buttons her shabby coat against the chill.
"Be a good girl! Night night! Sleep Tight!
Sweet dreams. I'll see you in the morning."

Grandma's off to make a Spitfire.
Grandma's off to work to win the war.

Geraldine Messenbird-Smith

Shell Shop

After running up and down years
of stairs, I'm in uniform again,
the trim black outline of me
lumped into grey dungarees.

Dust and smoke, day or night shift,
it's all the same without windows.
I try to colour myself –
an emerald turban, a ruby headscarf.

We all do. Look at us, scattered across
this old glove factory like so many parrots!
I don't know why our lips are juicy
with Auxiliary Red, as if we're longing

to kiss or be kissed.
Machines spit at us, hammers stutter.
We can't even speak. Alone
with the innards of cylinders,

their silver bellies open,
their blood-oil staining our hands
so we have to scrub them till they're raw.
I've still got ten fingers.

We touch our creations with such grace
you'd think we were sewing dresses of silk.
Under a shower of white-hot shavings
I cut the case into shape, twine the coils

and always, at the last stage, a bolt
tightens in my neck, sparks dance behind my eyes.
Then it's just me and the bomb.
The roar of a silence in which people go missing.

Anne Ryland

The Old Worcester Women, 1945

Calling over the carrot field
calling across the years
the old Worcester women in wartime

Is this one big enough for you dear
is this one big enough?

Young Elsie simpers
young Ivy smiles grim
Myrtle snorts a chortle
I titter *hee-hee*
we are
the young ladies of the carrot field
not joining in
not talking bawdy

Over the frosty field
to warm up the dawn
and is this one
big enough dear is this one
big enough for you?

Only one voice
genteelly
holds out
day after day

This one goes right
down to Austrilyer

Nothing would turn them though
from the subject in hand.

Gerda Mayer

Lowry's Women

I can still see the pinnied women, hair thick with cotton buds,
suddenly bursting out of factory doors
like discharged cannon, the whoops and swirls of laughter
frosting the air, their colourful coats
jostling for primacy at the rainbow hour;

the whole universe bursting with one intent;
the battle for bus seats on the great voyage home,
the sighs of relief watching the shores of terraced houses,
donkey stoned and primed with paint,
dip into the sea of the street.

And on the other side of the road, the enemy,
Delta spinners from The King standing at their stop
like lines of soldiers, their faces gripping the horizon
with the tenacity of their stare, watching us sail by
Shiloh Spinners on chariots wearing cotton in our hair.

Harriet Torr

Ponteland Chicken Factory 1969

The boy sat with his knife
and slashed those chickens north and south

they tumbled down the chutes
and an anointing scream rose from the women like pipes

playing their macabre tune, as the scrowed old ladies
bounced along the assembly line,

hung from hooks, clawed from below
by a plethora of hands and the guts chucked –

the steaming tray carried to a steely table
whilst the birds perambulated the room,

and I dug my cellophaned mitt
into the spirogyra of necks like willies

gizzards green with grit and bile
and livers hot with the bodies they'd come from.

Fifteen minutes of this of this made one woman sick
so we worked shifts –

the chickens still coming in on the mighty loom –
until washed, our hands acid with it (the gloves often off)

they were graded as A's – no bumps or bruises,
or B's – given to the women, the ones that had bled

whilst the C's – rotten even before they were dead –
disappeared.

At break in our eight-hour day for eight quid pay
(a week) we repaired with the women

to the back room where they ate sandwiches
made with the chickens they'd embalmed yesterday

and my friend Heather and me
well we drank the tea and ate bread and cheese

and counted our good fortune on being the girls
advanced to the chicken-grading, where we have remained.

Lynn Foote

In The Fish-House

The haddock blocks
easy gutting. It requires
longer than a holiday job to learn
the slick incisions
with the gutting-knife
about the three-pronged structure
of its back-bone.

The herring is simple
letting in
one deft stroke of the knife
along its belly
and releasing
its soft pinkish underworld
so easily
a new girl at the table
piles up gutted mounds
in her first afternoon

and at her feet
pails with scaly handles
fill up with
shoals of tiny tails
and heads brimful with eyes
and loads of flat back-bones.

Maureen Sangster

The Florist's Assistant

Each day her fingers bleed from picking thorns from
long-stemmed roses, for the sake of other people's
lovers, mothers; she takes her time to bruise and crush
the woody stalks of hothouse blooms, then strips the leaves
below the water line, takes tweezers to remove
each less than perfect petal, every bud gone blind.

For the *gone but not forgotten*, the *sadly missed*,
belov'd in this life, cherished in the next,
she stands on wet stone flags and leans her body
up against the workbench while she wires and hammers,
twists and binds, inhales chrysanthemums gone over,
day-old lilies and the fumes of waterlogged gypsophila.

Susan Utting

2

Filling the Kettle

You must find a thinning, a darker blue.
Raise the axe high above you.
Pretend the frozen lake is a moose head
or your oldest enemy.

You must pull the icy air sharp into your lungs.
Stretch your arms high.
Feel the cold like a knife, begin to hate
the weight of the metal above you.

Like an eagle weigh up distance.
The secret is confidence,
knowing the blade will land heavy,
will cut, not splinter.

You must build up a rhythm.
Soon you will not feel the bite
of each breath, the pain in your shoulders.
Soon you will see the glint of arctic waters.

Fiona Ritchie Walker

Shine

When the back door and the front door opened
you could see right through the house
to sky at the far end —
the doors lined up to make this corridor.
Every morning my mother got down
on her hands and knees
and polished the linoleum.
She pushed big rags around and sang
Danny Boy and *The Green Green Grass of Home*.
I helped, messing the words up
and sometimes, with my bum on a rag,
she would push me around like a boat.

Her work would come back to me
as I bathed her, knees of a penitent,
the swellings round each joint in her hands.
Five days into the coma there was the night
when her breathing calmed, to and fro,
I could feel her going, under the rhythm
beyond the room, across the plains
each paddock opening — she was so light.

The wind with its sound of doorways.
Somewhere at the end of the corridor
there was the morning sky, and the wind.
For days I will feel her there, housing and leaving.

Rhian Gallagher

The Visit

I

When my son lives in a house of his own
I will visit him.
I will drop my coat, hat and bags
on the floor,
just inside the door,
and demand to know when tea will be ready.

I will switch on the TV
to full volume,
and lie on the floor in my duvet
with a bowl of shredded wheat
milk to the brim
which, when empty,
I will slide under the settee.

I will shout at him
for tidying away my things,
refuse to sit up to the table
until my programme has finished
and say it is definitely not my turn
to help with the washing up.

II

When I arrive,
he welcomes me,
takes my coat,
ushers me into his tidy sitting room,
pours tea into thin china and offers me cake.
We talk like old friends.

Pauline Prior-Pitt

Detail

Kitchen Scene with Christ in the House of Martha and Mary 1618?
Diego Velázquez

White, fresh and heavy, eggs and their pellucid
membranes are chambers for yolk and albumen,
an embryonic universe. Pallid,
two moons gleam their reflection onto a spoon.

Brass pounding brass, pestle inside mortar
create cymbal sounds of *batterie de cuisine.*
Garlic colonizes the air, like river
or sea inundating land. From brine

come slippery bream for *dies veneris,*
who see their world through a watery
lens. Add olive oil and chop the chillies,
in these simple things there can be glory.

Martha adds salt and stirs this mixture slowly,
grills the fish and serves with the aioli.

Valerie Josephs

Mother Scrubbing the Floor

She had a dancer's feet, elegant, witty.
We had our father's, maverick spreaders of dirt.

Dirt from London, dirt from Kent,
Mud, dust, grass, droppings, wetness, things,
Dirt barefaced, dirt stinking, dirt invisible.

Whatever it was, she was ready:
The rubber kneeler, clanking galvanised bucket,
The Lifebuoy, the hard hot water.

Let me! we'd say, meaning *Hate to see you do this.*
Too old. Too resentful. Besides, you'll blame us
That you had to do it.

She never yielded. We couldn't do it right,
Lacking her hatred of filth, her fine strong hands.

Don't want you to do this, she said. *Don't want you to have to.*
Just remember this: love isn't sex
But the dreary things you do for the people you love.
Home is the girl's prison
The woman's workhouse, she said.
Not me, she said. *Shaw.*

I do remember. I stand where she knelt.

U A Fanthorpe

3

Numbers and Leaves

She's problem-solving in finite steps:
follicles / oocytes / fertilised zygotes
diminishing until the blank sheet
is thick with *multiple gestations /*
singleton pregnancies / failure to implant.
Each box reflecting through a tangle of green
the rates of miscarriage in women over 40
the numbers and leaves of the statistical tree.
Some of the windows are fixed and will not open.
But this is false, for any window
may be opened and become the future
chromosomal abnormality in twins, in triplets
the risks of amniocentesis to a healthy foetus.
The stories inside the house flicker with light.
She calculates the chances of *a take-home baby*
the child who waves from just one of those windows
so many rooms inhabited by grief.

Gerrie Fellows

Tall foreign doctor

She leans down from her gaunt height,
a crane in whose bill
storytellers have put kind words.

"Little women" she says
and their dark, slight bodies open.
Their vaginas are like torn flowers
to her hummingbird stitches.

Her foreign words clatter
like smooth stones.
Picked up
and dropped one by one,
each makes a small splash
in ears silted up
with fear and pain.

"It'll hurt
but you'll soon be better,
you'll go home in a new dress,
you'll marry again, have a live baby –
but *remember* – when your baby
starts walking inside you, *you* walk –
to the hospital."

Intimate as a scalpel
she first cuts into their frightened hearts,
lifts out panic, heavy as a tired child,
and lays it down,
stitches up their courage,
tall as a tree with shade.

Dark, delicate, scared,
small women
take fierce, giant steps over the harsh plateau
to clean sheets and a painful cure.

Easy to be a tree-like foreign doctor
bending down a long way
to peer at their child-ripped bodies.
But she won't stay foreign.

She wants with passion
like a rush of blood to her freckles
to speak as they do,
like a chuckle of water,
mouth to mouth, equal
and her bending to be
landscape, like the crane's.

Kate Foley

Yellow

'The banana!' You frown
over the objects on the table.
Then, your face an umber sun,
you lift the waxy crescent.
'What colour is it?'
A ripe 'oooh' of laughter,
hand flying in excitement
to the primrose headscarf that neatly
covers the dent in your skull;
and a waterfall of sounds carries
the rhythms and intonations of speech
though words are washed out.

For three years you've filled
time by painting – at first
lone, female figures
with ovals that didn't join up.
Now men and women dressed
in daffodil and scarlet perambulate
your paper world, and you are learning
to decode a few spoken words.

I didn't know the *you* you were
before the haemorrhage in your brain.
'Occupation: nurse' is a fact
filed away in a drawer.
Yet within the forest of damage
the essence remains of the you
who cornered beds with wit, wheeled in
kindness on the medicine trolley.

Outside: the mouthings of propaganda;
oil-troubled waters; the bitterness
of bombs. Here the news is:
you've read five words.
And now you're following my lips,
wavering towards the 'oo' of blue.
We take up your favourite colour,
chant it till the air around us
is leafed with our voices.
'Say it alone.' And you do:
'Ye-ll-ow.' The three petals
of sound fill the room.

Myra Schneider

The Headmistress

Her crenellated hair
rose solidly
above a stony front,
the knitted architecture
of her dresss
impressed with pillared cable,
stitches sprang
the awesome buttress of her chest.

She had made a fortress
of flesh,
each cell adhered
to the castle's code,
kept watch
against an unnamed foe.

Were the rooms
behind that impregnable brow
ever hung with silk?

The light in her windows
usually glinted
on arrows,
was it all drills and duties
or was there
occasional entertainment;
swigs of ale
from a keg of beer?

Isobel Thrilling

Homage to My Latin Teacher
for Mrs Stanley Hall

You swept into the lesson, dressed in red,
chalk dust powdering your hair, your patrician nose,
already translating Parkstone Grammar
First Form into AD 43:
our first taste of your noble, passionate tongue.

Salvete puellae! And we'd chant back
Salve domina! The exclamation mark
a chorus of chairs scraping the tiled floor
as we sat, a fizzing cohort of girls.

You rolled the words round your mouth and sucked
the juice out of them. I hid at the back
and watched you spit. Like a mother bird,
you fed us from your own lips – *the table;*
to the table; by, with, from the table.

And so I learnt to unravel the puzzle
of the 'Unseen', marvel at the precision
of syntax and rhetoric, recognise
the English in the squares of the mosaic.

We could all have cheered at Cicero's coaxing,
wept when Dido flung herself on the pyre,
but knew that someone had to found Rome
or else we'd have no baths, no straight roads,
no alphabet from which to build our own.

Your daughter was in the year above mine.
I wondered how it would be to have you
as a mother; if you talked Latin at home.

Linda France

Miss Jenkins' Lesson

Miss Jenkins bulled P.E.
Her hockey voice made wall bars shake,
first-formers shiver. Between
divided skirt and ankle socks
were calves that could have been
umbrella stands, thighs
that would crush a man, if any
had been brave enough to try.

Miss Jenkins forced our purple gooseflesh
out of doors, lacrossed or netballed us,
made numbed joints sweat. Or else
we bounced on rubber mats,
jerked over beams and horses,
scorched down ropes.

Miss Jenkins watched us strip
and herded our pubescence
through the showers. Jets needled us,
feet slithered. We were made to dance
hard pacing circles, water pummelled.

Miss Jenkins smiled, white slabs
over-toothing her mouth.
She leered until last aertex vest,
last teen bra, last green knickers
vanished under gymslips. At last
she locked her private cloakroom door
and ran her own shower long and long.

Even then her loud gasps
above the whooshing of the water
punctuated whispers
of twenty fascinated schoolgirls.

Alison Chisholm

Woman Writing

A woman writes at a desk in a study. Furiously
awake at five a new theorem buzzing, she constructs it
with her pen – *Thermodynamics and the Heartbeats of Tree-
Frogs in Sarawak*. Her hair is electromagnetic:
why brush it, it is white thought. Behind her a model:
molecules, a tree of them, primaries, red, yellow.

Today is blue. She allows it to happen. This is not
a woman writing her memoirs. She is writing off the edge
of the planet. What mirror? What toothpaste?

She is newly painted vibrant criss-cross dashes:
her sweater, glasses, the lines on her face.
This hour could have been a century blasting
away a stockade of men in white coats.
Today she is eighty-five. So much to do. So far to go.

Pam Thompson

Part 4

Women Speak Out

Out of the huts of history's shame
I rise
Up from a past that's rooted in pain
I rise

Maya Angelou

Weird Sister

Dark is dangerous,   don't go into the forest;
it's never your turn;   come back from always.

Females are labyrinths,   ladders, trample-spaces,
receptive stigmas,   beatific latencies.

She trails meaning like the Milky Way,
suffers the law of limits,   writes in white ink.

Enjoined to silence,   she is its image,
a wraith-like Madonna   in an ivory cameo.

Self-abnegation is her fate;   she's a State prisoner
denied all access;   appease, propitiate!

Woman is negative,   eternally the Other,
an incidental being,   a supernumerary bone.

Battling for freedom   from the blasted heath,
the cradle is her matrix and the womb her burning.

Joan Condon

Some People
for Eoin

Some people know what it's like,

to be called a cunt in front of their children
to be short for the rent
to be short for the light
to be short for school books
to wait in the Community Welfare waiting-rooms full of smoke
to wait two years to have a tooth looked at
to wait another two years to have a tooth out (the same tooth)
to be half strangled by your varicose veins but you're
198th on the list
to talk into a banana on a jobsearch scheme
to talk into a banana in a jobsearch dream

to be out of work
to be out of money
to be out of fashion
to be out of friends
to be in for the Vincent de Paul man
to be in space for the milk man
(sorry, mammy isn't in today she's gone to Mars for the weekend)
to be in Puerto Rico this week for the blanket man
to be in Puerto Rico next week for the blanket man
to be dead for the coal man
(sorry, mammy passed away in her sleep, overdose of coal
in the tea-pot)
to be in hospital unconscious for the rent man
(St Jude's ward, 4th floor)
to be second-hand
to be second class
to be no class
to be looked down on
to be walked on
to be pissed on
to be shat on

and other people don't.

Rita Ann Higgins

Quite a Day

You didn't say you liked my house.
You just sat down, asking questions,
legs crossed at the ankles, removing
the toddler's hands from your clip-board.
I had washed the coloured crayon marks
off the walls for you, and scrubbed
the rush matting so it smelled as sweet
as summertime in far away Norfolk,
and herded the cats into the garden
so they shouldn't tear your tights.

Cohabiting, you said, as if it was
a gobstopper stuck in your throat.
The baby sat in the cats' basket
and chewed on a piece of paper
looking gormless. The whole house
looked gormless and done for and shabby,
so very market stall, so very Co-op.
I even felt ashamed of Vermeer's
poor lace-maker, eternally bent over
her work with her high forehead under
the braided and parted hair.

I see, you said, you have a typewriter.
Like owning a rattlesnake, you made it seem.
Do I co-habit with the typewriter?
Do I cook the cats when the allowance is gone?
Do I, hell, do I? No, the children's father
has not married me. Studying for a degree,
you said, and twitched your skirt over
your virginal bottom as you pranced through
the hall and over the grubby Oxfam mat,
neatly dressed with your navy-blue hat.

'Go way', shouted the toddler, 'go way.'
His first linked words. It was quite a day.

Elizabeth Bartlett

Name

In time he lost her name, settled on You and Her.
She. The anonymity of gender.
Her mother too, summoned by nods,
by impatient, sideways eyes, by clicking fingers.

She wasn't pink and pretty, more denim than lace.
Not pigeonholed, he couldn't place her,
easier to ignore her as she slipped in and out of days
from clean to dirty and back again, like laundry.

He breathed her brothers like pure oxygen,
illuminating the very air with their names.
Beneath the quilt, she repeated and repeated hers
until she thought she might choke.

One morning he didn't waken,
stayed in bed, cold gristle, bone and cartilage,
while in the yellow kitchen and neon bright bathrooms –
cooking and soaping, unaware it was a death day.

At the wake she reclaimed her name,
dangled it above the coffin where he lay,
still not looking at her, still not seeing her.

Lesley Quayle

The Ghost of My Mother Comforts Me
after Van Morrison

Do not fear, daughter,
when they lift their sticks, their stones,
when they hiss beneath their breaths –

*Fallen woman, adultress, breaker of marriage vows
made before a holy priest to an honourable man.*

For you, daughter, there is no blame,
for you no portion of guilt,
for you're made in my likeness.
You can take the crucifixion from your voice.
I will stroke your forehead till you sleep,
till you pass over into the dreamworld
where we can walk together in gardens wet with rain
or fly along old star roads
or sit quietly near running water.

And when you wake refreshed
you'll be ready for their sticks, their stones,
their names that cannot hurt you.
Balance your gypsy soul, lodged
in the body given you, my daughter,
for your pleasure and as a tool for struggle,
against the weight of the world's troubles.
Take comfort in the knowledge that you are not alone.
There are many like you on the earth,
and you will be numbered among the warriors
when the great book is written.

Because I am your mother I will protect you
as I promised you in childhood.
You will walk freely on the planet,
my beloved daughter. Fear not
the lightning bolts of a Catholic god, or any other,
for I have placed my body and my soul between you and all harm.

Paula Meehan

Lilith

No one's child hunkers down beside a stream, elbows stuck out.
She's impersonating birds.
She thinks if she can get the angle right,
If she can believe hard enough,
She will become a bird,
A thing of grace with bones lighter than feathers.
She imagines her plumage, a ruffle of fluffy down feathers,
A slick cover of iridescent colours, rippling like water.
Her feet will shrink. The skin will turn hard.
Her claws will grip the ground.
Instead of a telltale face she'll have a mask,
Her secrets locked behind stupid eyes.
No one will try to guess which man she most resembles.
The blank space on her birth certificate will no longer matter:
It's just paper, it will burn.
And she, too, will burn:
Not growing pains at all, she'll make herself anew.
From a girl with muck on her face and sour-smelling hair
She'll become a red bird, howling,
Ascending from the golden egg, unfathered
And unmothered, her wings made of light and dirt.
From dirt we are born
And to dirt we shall return.

Helen Kitson

Signing Him Away

For eighteen years I waited for his call,
And when it came
I feared his voice. I heard the same brutal
Seduction, the same
Dark timbre. Double pain.

And I'd be lacking all the qualities
Surrounding him:
No clever turn of phrase, no sparkling speech
To wallpaper my shame,
No childhood clichés.

No day without a thought for him, always
Regret at signing
Him away. Oh, but his eyes
Would burn and sting,
Would sue my dreams,

Would claim his other life, and mine.
I sit here trembling
Waiting for his face, not knowing
How to mime the mother role, dreading
His footfall and the ring

I cannot answer.

Lotte Kramer

Smile for Daddy

At last he is quiet; his harsh words
can no longer scare the living daylights
out of me. I never understood the story
they told me of him in hospital asking
to see me, dressed in my new brown coat,
aged three or four. Today I wear my black.
Bartletts as far as the eye can see pack
the crematorium pews. Don't nick the books
of Common Prayer, the gilded lettering pleads.
He would have liked to see us all walking
in the rain behind a gun-carriage, his medals
lying on the polished coffin lid,
a sort of mini state funeral, the slow drums,
the tolling bells, the black veils.

He fought, but did not bleed or die
for his country, as he disciplined
but did not love his children.
Smile for Daddy. Somewhere there's a face
grimacing at a window, a small girl held high
in the air, a pale hand waving weakly.
All the men I've loved knock on wood,
and seem to wear his humourless stare,
used me for bayonet practice, went absent
without leave, could reduce me to tears,
as he did, but they were not aware
of this, and so we wait for him to disappear,
silenced at last, although not in my dreams,
but that is my funeral, not his.

Elizabeth Bartlett

Charcot's Pet

Before my voice disappeared
like a rabbit up a sleeve
I wanted to be a singer
in the Folies Bergère.

The doctor is a kind man:
he keeps me warm,
he feeds me seed cake
and assam tea.

But sometimes he makes me crawl.
Pick up the crumbs
my little goose.

At night I lie beside him
more silent than a blade of grass.
I allow his cold fingertips
to circle my heart.

Tomorrow, he says,
I must rehearse for the show
in the auditorium of the Saltpêtrière.
The doctors will love me!

He has made me a hat
of peacock feathers.
He has taught me to bark.

When he stares into my eyes
he can make me do anything.

But he can't make me sing.

Maggie Sawkins

Jean-Martin Charcot, the first of the great European theorists of hysteria, frequently
staged 'shows' to the members of his neurological service at the Saltpêtrière Hospital.
Blanche Whitman, Charcot's pet hysteric, was one of the main attractions.

Not Your Muse

I'm not your muse, not that creature
in the painting, with the beautiful body,
Venus on the half-shell. Can
you not see I'm an ordinary woman
tied to the moon's phases,
bloody six days in twenty-eight? Sure

I'd like to leave you in love's blindness,
cherish the comfort of your art, the way
it makes me whole and shining,
smooths the kinks of my habitual distress,
never mentions how I stumble into the day,
fucked up, penniless, on the verge of whining

at my lot. You'd have got away with it
once. In my twenties I often traded a bit
of sex for immortality. That's a joke.
Another line I swallowed, hook
and sinker. Look at you –
rapt, besotted. Not a gesture that's true

on that canvas, not a droopy breast,
wrinkle or stretchmark in sight.
But if it keeps you happy who am I
to charge in battledressed to force you test
your painted doll against the harsh light
I live by, against a brutal merciless sky.

Paula Meehan

Massacre

(from a sequence)

> 'Un monceau de platras s'accumule au milieu de mon atelier, c'est
> un veritable sacrifice humain'.....Camille Claudel

Preparing for the unburiable act of burial
at the back of her blackest mirrors,
she takes out axe and mallet and lines up

her sculptures which stare her out, claiming
to be part of her which, as part of him,
exists no longer. Prepared for the sacrifice

and without emotion, she steadily thwacks.
Profile, limb, torso. No blood is let.
The percussive blows accompany dances

of nerve-endings on the spot. Even chips
and jagged defacements have the power,
still, to pain and to resist the flames

of the stubborn passion against which
she warms her toes. Last cries of accidental souls
quickened in her works by the sweep of him

revive the torchlight, limelight and midnights
when he prowled around her with an artist's aim.
Like a spectator, staring herself out, now,

she cancels the carter hired to inter the remains,
and, leaving behind no address, her key
under the doormat, she goes off to piece together,

in her head, the ashes she has made, full
of ghosts of failed promises and old spells.
No one will see her in strange cities digging up

paving stones indented by anonymous feet –
to be carried home upon her back counter-signed
and ingrown. No one will listen to the women

bent on her acclaim, untethering ages from stone.

Patricia McCarthy

Camille Claudel, 1864-1943, the French sculptor, sister of Paul Claudel, was Rodin's
model and passionate mistress. When he refused to leave his wife to marry her, her
depression was so great that she destroyed her sculptures in the flat where she lived,
before being committed to a lunatic asylum where she never sculpted again.

Four women wed

But on that night, that Hallowe'en,
a hex came down
upon their heads, their marriage beds.
And in due course,
the first bride turned into – a horse.

Her husband was a farming man,
soon had her harnessed to his plough.
All through the muddied, earth-bound years
she dragged the day round, by his side,
his plodding creature, bridled bride.

The second turned into a dog.
Ran at her husband's booted heel,
his bitch, his slave, his Ariel;
obeying every curt command,
to sit or fetch or lick his hand –
no matter how he kicked, how cruel.

The third became a charming cat.
She walked alone, but sometimes sat
clever and clean, upon his lap,
and let his conjuring fingers lift
the purr from her, content with that.
His lovely, his familiar cat.

The fourth became a blossoming tree,
and in his house she stood so tall
she broke his roof, and broke as well
his jealous heart. He groaned, he swore
to cut her down, to break the spell,
then in her branches, saw and heard
a singing bird.

He stayed his hand.
And still she grew. The blossoms blew.
He searched for fruit and found it good,
so by the by, he grew content
to lie beneath her, looking to
the blest, the magical sky.

Ann Alexander

The Pow Wow Café

To buy herself a new 50's moderne sofa
and wrought iron-framed repro of Picasso's
'Don Quixote' my father was too much
of a tightwad to buy her, my mother
got a job at the Pow Wow Café, a
truckstop on Highway 19 in Downey,
California where the waitresses wore
short, short red polka-dot skirts and
low-cut white peasant blouses that showed
half of my mother's baba au rum breasts
'No!' bellowed my father while my mother
ironed her starched uniform into stiff
Mt. Everest peaks, not speaking to him
for trying to tell her what to do.
'No!' he bellowed as she drove away
to work her first night at the Pow Wow Café
and my father put up with this for
four nights, chainsmoking, biting his
fingernails, watching tv and come Friday night
he took my mother's short, short skirt
and low-cut peasant blouse and me to the
Pow Wow Café where he threw open the
manager's office door and threw my mother's
uniform onto the floor and bellowed,
'My wife's not working in this
whorehouse any more!' and then my father
sat down at the counter with all the truckers
ordered a chocolate sundae for me, coffee,
double cream, for himself, and told the
waitress when she brought them how nice
she looked this evening.

Joan Jobe Smith

111

Thanksgiving, October 1970

You at Whiffen Spit, on the seaward side,
where the Cascade Mountains rise
in sheeted skies, like the demented
ghosts of wedding cakes, where hawks
and turkey vultures flay the air.

Too quiet, our children's play
in this graveyard of the sea. Pensive,
they sift the bleached bones of cuttlefish
and conch, find a calcified starfish,
ask me why it doesn't swim.

You move to the harbour side, examine
sheltered rock pools, where small fish
dart and hide in seaweed gardens,
find a sea anemone, a pulsating cell, red
as a woman's vulva and poke it with a stick.

Later, in the shell called home,
you strip me, tie me, throw me down,
kneel between my quivering knees,
thrust screwdrivers into my womb,
skewer the woman from the girl.

June English

Witnesses

We three in our dark decent clothes,
unlike ourselves, more like the three
witches, we say, crouched over the only
ashtray, smoke floating into our hair,

wait. An hour; another hour.
If you stand up and walk ten steps
to the glass doors you can see her there
in the witness box, a Joan of Arc,

straight, still, her neck slender,
her lips moving from time to time
in reply to voices we can't hear:
'I put it to you ... I should like to suggest ...'

It's her small child who is at stake.
His future hangs from these black-clad
proceedings, these ferretings under her sober
dress, under our skirts and dresses

to sniff out corruption: 'I put it to you
that in fact your husband ... that my client ...
that you yourself initiated the violence ...
that your hysteria ...' She sits like marble.

We pace the corridors, peep at the distance
from door to witness box (two steps up,
remember, be careful not to trip
when the time comes) and imagine them there,

the ones we can't see. A man in a wig
and black robes. Two other men
in lesser wigs and gowns. More men
in dark suits. We sit down together,

shake the smoke from our hair, pass round
more cigarettes (to be held carefully
so as not to smirch our own meek versions
of their clothing), and wait to be called.

Fleur Adcock

Jury

I'd noticed her hands before, large and quiet
in her lap as she listened through all the words
for the sound she wanted, the call from her scrap
of daughter, fed on demand
while we waited

and I thought of how she'd hold that feather-weight
in one hand while the other cupped the warm head
with its beating fontanelle close to her breast
as if that soft suck and tug
were all the world

and she could forget the knife, (one of a set),
with the serrated edge we'd seen already,
an ordinary kitchen knife, its ten-inch blade
nestling securely inside
a cling-wrapped box.

But it was the photo made me cry – her hand,
in colour, the palm flat for the camera,
fingers stretched apart to show the base of each
cut to the bone, ragged wounds
only half healed:

how painful it must have been to open out
the sheltering fist, uncurl her fingers and feel
the tight scabs crack, exposed for an indifferent
photographer to record
the naked truth.

And the moment all the others led up to
and away from – the moment before her hand
lost its grip on a handle made slippery with
his blood, slid down the blade? – that,
we couldn't see.

Mary MacRae

3

Woman

In this no-man's land she stands tall,
a giantess among giant trees
whose canopies shield from fierce sky.
I'm hooked by eyes that arc dark suns.
"Why have you come to me, woman?"

'Because you are rooted far in the past,
because you bore the one who bore me,
because your rolling voice is ocean,
because your hundred arms hold out
the mothering I've always longed for.'

"But you are blessed with love, woman,
live the life you've chosen and you've found
words, the whole rainbow of words."

'Wise One,' I lean forward to ask more
but her body's thinned – I can see her ribs.
Her face is darkening, her voice sharpening.

> I was only ten when I was given
> to a husband. He raped me day after day.
> The first time pain tore through me...

> I was thrown into prison and had to trade
> sex for food which would fill my belly.
> Even when I was in labour I was shackled...

> I was bought by a man who sells my body
> every day... At gunpoint I was told to pound
> a baby. If I'd refused they'd have killed me too...

> I was distraught when they ordered me
> to marry him. To punish me they emptied
> acid on my face. I was burnt. I almost died...

Grief and fury leap up, overwhelm me.
'What can I do?' I cry. A flutter
of scarf or leaf, a whisper in my head:
"Woman, you have words. Speak, write."

Myra Schneider

A Litany

after Michael Longley

I cannot name for you all the wildflowers
of the Machars I saw in one day, but I can tell you
that among them were sea campion and spring squill,
herb robert, burnet rose and scarlet pimpernel,
bugle, bluebell, cranesbill, speedwell,
sea radish and birdsfoot trefoil, eyebright and thrift,
red campion and ramson, primrose and violet

and I can tell you that at the end of the rocky shore
in the cave of Ninian, bringer of Christianity
there were laid little wilted bunches of these flowers
along with crosses made of driftwood
tied with scraps of rope or fishing net,
and smooth pebbles left by pilgrims.

I cannot name for you all the women of that place
killed as witches or as covenanters, but I can tell you
that among them were Helen Moorhead and Jean Thomson,
Agnes Comenes and Agnes Clerk, Elspeth Thomson and Elspeth McEwen,
Margaret Clark, Margaret Wilson, Margaret Maclachlan,
Janet Dunn, Janet Corsone, Janet Callan, Janet McMurdoch,
Janet McKendrig and Janet McGowane

and I can tell you that perhaps a sister or a friend
of one of these accused slipped down Physgill Glen at dusk
and made her way to the cave, even then when pilgrimages
were banned, and made supplication to the saint
and brought for him a pebble and a handful of wildflowers
she'd gathered and whose names she knew by heart.

Elizabeth Burns

116

Forgive Us Our Bodies

In 1942 mother was 'churched',
sent back clean to her anxious mother
after the bloody business of bearing me.
Some years later, I met the vicar – small, bald,
superior, quoting Bertrand Russell.

He was the mumbler of mumbo jumbo
who cleansed my mother, purified her
of the flux of blood that came with birth,
that left a taint, made her untouchable,
until he prayed in his Selwyn College voice.

Later still, I learned through my work
how women with knives spud out the clitoris
of young African girls, leave them tight, sore,
sometimes in high fever, maimed, barren.
And though it happens female circumcision

was not in the book of the little, cocksure
vicar of St. John's, he was some way
down the road of fearing mother's clitoris,
knowing she would always be too dirty
to serve as holy priest or bishop

turning a blind eye if godmothers,
with knives under thick clothes, with threats
and promises, with the strong arms of old women,
had drawn girls to, say, the Yorkshire moors,
and closed their wounds with thorns?

Dilys Wood

sometimes the practice was to 'sew up' these wounds with strong thorns

The Killer Woman

Sometimes she uses her teeth,
that old Killer Woman,
she spits out a swill of blood and flesh
and where she hawks, the vultures swarm.

I almost died,
held down by my mother,
sliced with a blood caked razor,
blood and dirt and flies,
my world a sour and stinking voyage
into pain.

She ravelled up the wound,
a torque of thorns
and laced my legs tight and still.
My tongue burst from its root,
my heart thundered like a drumskin
as I fetched up life in the slow, writhing heat.

I have run through the shifting desert,
adrift where the light is not broken,
away from the dead-eyed Killer Woman
with her rituals of razor and teeth,
and the men of the tribe who burn for me now,
cauterized, impenetrable,
reconstructed for their particular pleasure,
and my vocation shines before me like a bright eye.

Lesley Quayle

(Waris Dirie was born into a tribe of Somalian desert nomads. She was circumcised, aged
five, and almost died. Fleeing an arranged marriage at twelve, she trekked through the
desert for six days and nights. In her teens she became a super model and in her twenties
was appointed an ambassador for the UN with a mission to rid Africa of ritual female
circumcision).

Katya

Not of my own choosing
Do my paps darken like muzzles.
My belly slowly swells.
I cannot see my valley now.
I crave for lassi
But they bring us rusty water
In the bottom of a can.

They come and come,
Day, night, day,
Unbuttoning
As the door slaps against the stucco.
They leave our thighs and faces
Crusty with their stink.

And after me,
They hump across on to my mother,
Covering her shrunken face
With her heavy dirndl skirt.
She is dry, dry.
Her womb is a husk.

Each day I am ripening.
I do not want this cuckoo
Fluttering its rabid wings
In my darkness.
I can see its wild eyes beneath my skin.
It will suck me dry as rock.

Yet, I have practised its birth –
How I will keep my legs far apart,
My eyes screwed shut,
Then roll it with my heel in the dust
Kicking it and its afterbirth
Down the mountainside.

Or, how I will say, *Give me my baby,*
And boy or girl, call it Katya.
That was my mother's name.

Pat Borthwick

A Photograph Seen When I Was Twelve

There were women of all ages
their shoulders bunched forward,
running before guards with pistols,
dogs, long coats with high collars.

– You know now, so why say more?

One hand thrown across her breasts,
the other thrown across her mound of Venus,
dark-haired, thick like the dishevelled
dark hair round her staring face.

I can't forget these Venuses of the earth,
fat, flabby, crouching before blows.

Standing hidden behind a thick pine trunk,
smelling its resin in the cold,
my nose pressed to the barbed wire,
blobs of snow falling without lightness,
licking the high collar of my dirty mac.

I opened the book and looked at the picture,
closed it in shame, opened it, closed it,
opened it, stared at the women,
not millions, there were ten of them

who ran in the perishing cold
beyond the barbed wire and the pine trunk
(into which I pressed myself with disbelief).
They ran on out of my line of vision,
they were prodded beyond.

I left their naked bodies and stared
at their faces, and, running, their eyes
eyed me back; the small round woman
in front, she had wavy ragged hair
and broad cheeks, the next was slender
with arched nose – The prints were very bad.

Yet I insisted, huddling my piled clothing
behind the pine tree and the barbed wire,
I know her, I shouted, caught on hooks,
she works behind the till in the store,
curtly dealing out change as she says –

120

how's the family; and the one with
the fine bones is my history teacher
whose calm desire to be objective,
to wait carefully for the examination results
of history, I argue with passionately.

Her fine dark blonde hair is wrenched out,
everything gone. I couldn't burst out, turn,
nothing and no one. Not I, no one,
to rip the guards out cold
from their barbed wire costumes.

Only that since then at the border
I have stood naked, and look forever
at these hardly discernible women's faces,
who were the queens of their bodies
until the final day, and shall be;
though they were taken from themselves.

Judith Kazantzis

The Blue Apron

A rare thing hung in a glass case,
Like an open wing strung out between pins,
It was a shroud,
Mended *ad infinitum,*
The distilled rising of a cloud,
Butterflies bearing up the dead.
How did this map of tenderness survive?
A patchwork apron hewn with a needle and thread.
An old Gestapo *Kino* plays films about Terezin.
For what I did not know, I cannot mourn,
Yet unformed words are beginning to form...
It was as pale as dried cornflowers,
Bleached to a gossamer sail in places,
The stitches like railway tracks over blue fields.

Jehane Markham

German Woman, 1945

The war ran into me, like all women.
It made me a light tin spoon.
I was stranded among them,
Soldaten, Soldaten.
I wore a shawl of cloud-coloured wool.
I lived hard by.
How little their marching mattered to me.
Their laughter bruised my bones.

Gillian Allnutt

Releasing the Enemy

My German partner opens the bidding,
'Two Hearts': above her, stiff portraits
Of her ancestors, not a smile among them.
I had resented her Prussian background,
Her railings against the Russians.

They pillaged her grandfather's farm,
Dragged him into the wood,
Shots … silence …
She and her sisters refugees.
I had heard that story years ago,
Only today it penetrates my soul.
'Two Hearts', a strong call.

Anne Kind

Amputee
(Photograph from an exhibition on women and war)

Poised as a Benin bronze, her head's proud angle
the first thing I notice, next
the calm of her hands. She seems to cup sunlight
between folded palms. As I come close
her gaze travels through me. I can't read it.

When I become aware her flowered frock
hides neither her slender right leg nor
its clumsy wooden mockery on the left
I don't know what I feel. Is it shock?
Distaste she's let herself be made a peepshow?

No. Curiously she seems complete
seated in massive repose
like an Egyptian deity. One who knows
in every fibre human cruelty,
rough human kindness. Meets both with grace.

A. C. Clarke

4

The Fathers

The fathers are losing their power to harm us.

See the long line of daddies falling like ninepins.

One was a banker; his stocks and shares are shrunk.
One was a farmer; his land has been razed.
One was a priest; his altars lie abandoned.

Where do they go, the daddies, when they keel over?

Nicola Slee

"What Do Women Want?"

I want a red dress.
I want it flimsy and cheap,
I want it too tight, I want to wear it
until someone tears it off me.
I want it sleeveless and backless,
this dress, so no one has to guess
what's underneath. I want to walk down
the street past Thrifty's and the hardware store
with all those keys glittering in the window,
past Mr. and Mrs. Wong selling day-old
donuts in their café, past the Guerra brothers
slinging pigs from the truck and onto the dolly,
hoisting the slick snouts over their shoulders.
I want to walk like I'm the only
woman on earth and I can have my pick.
I want that red dress bad.
I want it to confirm
your worst fears about me,
to show you how little I care about you
or anything except what

I want. When I find it, I'll pull that garment
from its hanger like I'm choosing a body
to carry me into this world, through
the birth-cries and the love-cries too,
and I'll wear it like bones, like skin,
it'll be the goddamned
dress they'll bury me in.

Kim Addonizio

There's Something About A Woman Swallowing Flames

She kicks her head back: if you're quick
you spot the hunted fox in her eyes
before it goes to ground. She is diamond tonight
or something decked out as diamond. She spins
so fast you're trapped in her sleight of hand,
dazzles fire and ice in a fever of smiles.
You don't think she can do this, her skin is paper-thin
and her hair crackles with static. Her torches hurl
through the air, juggle saffron, electric blue, flame.
Colours skelter up and down the sharp tongues. Spit.
Curse. Bite at the ceiling, the oh so flammable curtains.
A flick of her wrists and the firesnakes
race for her throat, home in on the blaze
under her breastbone. The air catches its breath.
Light fizzes from the copper hair, the copper fingertips.
Your eyes want to bolt for the door,
sidle home but are held in check.
You scent the quick musk of vixen.
She fills the room.

Jennie Osborne

Heading for the Heights

Why did she seek out the mountains –
January, force nines yelling,
the black bog, minimal tracks rained out,
the waterfall iced solid?

Where all sane people were boarded up,
not daring to venture far from
their hot pipes, when her children called –
why need she go? What drove her?

The same, perhaps, that drives me from
the car-infested valleys,
to climb, till only the ancient pack-roads
are left, on top of the world.

You see them, heading for the heights,
on most mornings this winter,
equipped, you think, for the long haul –
maps, snow-boots and compass.

Wander all night. Doctors and missionaries
untraced, lone farms inaccessible;
how easy, on the calmest day,
to lose your track and perish.

Each year the bodies lie unclaimed,
and some, never discovered.
Yet still they head for the high ground,
no child's crying will stop them.

Merryn Williams

Building Chapel Jane

They call it the thin chapel, *Chapel Moen*,
in their speech. They say I cannot lift its weight in rock.
If boulders are too big I will bring small stones.
I will carry them further. I will carry more.

They say, if I were a man I could do it, but a woman
cannot tend chapel. Eve must not slot herself
between men and God. They fling words
like mouldy apples as if I were in the stocks.

They have not thought – a woman gives birth,
is mistress of renewal. Let them shed me
like a snake's skin. Here, where the world's edge
plunges into the sea's cold mouth

and streams rattle between twists of fallen cliff,
my soul is with the stonechat on his open perch.

Jenny Hamlett

The name Jane derives from the Cornish *moen* (thin). The medieval chapel is on the wild
north coast towards Land's End and was built of small stones.

Bone China

I want to leave something behind
like the maid who cracked one night
the length of her heart,
who crept shaking down the staircase
to where the service shone on the dresser,
plates pale as a row of moons.

She stacked them in her arms –
a weight greater than all she owned –
bore their white tower to the kitchen garden
where she stood between the soft fruit beds
and smashed each one against the wall
with a planetary anger.

That dawn she walked out of her story forever,
though her flavour salted the servants' tongues for months,
and clearing the ground a hundred years later
of this self-seeded scrub of ash
I can still piece bits of her together – white and sharp –
as if the earth were teething.

Esther Morgan

Maud Speaking

When I came to the gate alone
　You were making eyes at a lily,
Conversing in such an intimate tone
　That I felt remarkably silly.
Your grotesque behaviour I cannot condone.
　Your welcome I found chilly.

A poet, I know, may be queer:
　One learns to be dignified.
One would rather not interfere.
　One has one's feminine pride.
That very long poem about Mr Arthur Henry Hallam
　One took in one's stride.

But a man who talks all night
　To a larkspur and a rose –
Is something wrong with your sight?
　I thought you meant to propose,
But when I arrived you ignored me quite.
　I might as well have been prose.

And I didn't care for the stuff
  You wrote about my head;
Little head, like a light-minded bit of fluff;
  But I'm tolerably well-read,
Would have studied at Newnham, under Miss Clough,
  If Papa hadn't sworn *better dead.*

Away, melancholy!
  Lord Tennyson, goodbye.
I'm up to here with botany,
  I want someone streetwise and spry.
There are plenty of suitable fish in the sea.
  Poets need not apply.

U A Fanthorpe

Larks

Who says larks are happy?
Maybe they sing to scare off marauders
or to drown the pleading cries of babies.
Perhaps it's simply what they do.
In prison melodies are sounds that fill the cell
brim-full bursting with noise that pushes
against all four walls like a crowd of friends
each pressing her palm hard against one scarred surface
so the cell is not empty, its one voice not alone.
People in cells sing their sounds
through walls into corridors that funnel them
like an orchestral score with no conductor.
Kenney, Lytton and the Pankhursts sang in Holloway
the old warrior's march that on better days
rang through embattled streets and pushed hard
against the underside of grim clouds lifting
their weight for an instant as green and purple
sashes caught the light. Women joined in
perhaps happy,   perhaps not
but they sang like the obstinate lark
knowing what they must do to reach clear sky
as the brooding clouds moved aside the like the slow
rhythmic swinging open of the cell's door.

Judith Barrington

Chipko – 1978

We set off singing and with drums
close together in the pre-dawn grey
summon courage on the winding path.

Our feet talk to the dry cracked earth
where other trees once stood. Dust
blows determination in our eyes and mouths.

I lay my cheek against the knobbly bark
wrap arms around its years of growth
listen to sap rising, leaf-speak, green,

try not to see Amrita Devi, axed down
with her arms about a tree. My small heart
set against the strength of money.

The loggers are felled to silence at the sight:
bright saris flower against each dark trunk;
the forest, a garden of women.

Maggie Butt

(The Chipko movement saved a Himalayan forest from being cut down for tennis
rackets.)

The White Bird

for Anna Akhmatova

How marvellously you squandered yourself,
Anna Andreevna, your Tatar bearing
royal in a casual shawl, and wearing
a ring that was a gift of the moon.

Always a witch not a wife, in the house
of three husbands your most
adulterous love was for
the poems they didn't want written

and you could never abandon.
Even as the gay sinner of Tsarskoye Selo,
the future cast its shadow into your heart.
Tonight, I drink to your ruined house,

loneliness, and that white bird
you chose instead of happiness.

Elaine Feinstein

Motherhood

Suppose I emptied my flat of everything,
everything but my books? The elephants
would have to go. They'd be the first to go
– being the youngest – and the last, the plants
perhaps, relics of early motherhood.
I'd keep the piano, all my files and photos.

I'd keep my grandmother's chest to keep my photos
in, in and not on top of, everything
swept absolutely clear of motherhood.
Nothing shall move: no herd of elephants
proceed down my mantelpiece, spider-plants
produce babies, carpets moths, moths shall go

into the ether where all bad spells go.
I'm sick of the good. Of drooling over photos
that lie, lie, lie, breaking my back over plants
for whom - *Oh! for whom?* Not everything
I thought green greened. Not even elephants
consoled me for the bane of motherhood.

Therefore motherhood must go. Motherhood
must go as quietly as prisoners go
and all her things go with her, elephants
troop behind her, tapestries drown her, photos –
OK photos can stay but everything
dust-collecting goes the way of the plants.

Everything shall live in name only. Plants
now extinct shall be extolled, motherhood
shall be blessed but not mothers, everything
everywhere being their fault though they go
to the dock protesting, producing photos
of happy toddlers, citing elephants,

rashly, as preceptors since elephants,
however vicious they may be to plants
or rear dangerously when threatened with photos,
are the very model of motherhood.
Such are the myths of nature. They shall go.
There shall be room, time, space, for everything:

room in the wild for elephants and plants;
time to go rummaging a chest for photos;
space for everything cleared of motherhood.

Mimi Khalvati

Part 5

Love Relationships

Home

When you held me
A river poured through me:
From the base of my spine to my scalp
It flooded me,
The beginning to the end of time;

And in that moment
I was a bright salmon
Leaping upstream, against the current
With all my might,
Making my long way home.

Katrina Porteous

The Firefly Cage

I carry the firefly cage
a calligraphy of willow
scribed into shape;
search among the stalks
of mangrove and bamboo
tease out the fireflies,
lifting them tenderly
stroking the dark lacquer shells.
Our dead Emperors brood
over us, their white caps
peaked with snow.

I have watched the fireflies:
the female sits on her elevated perch
the male times his signal
executes his exotic lantern pavan.
They meet and mate
their lights synchronise.
Sometimes a female imposter
makes fraudulent response.
I have found her devouring
his flesh; his light glows,
her light is carnivorous-bright.

My Master leads me into
the garden beyond the pagoda,
the sky washed pale as wisteria.
I carry the firefly cage,
loop it onto a branch of camellia.
We are caught in its halo
a leaf is detached by my clumsiness;
he shudders, sees images of death.
He is grave, I am solemn; he unpins
my black hair, unwinds
the sash of my kimono.
We sway in a hammock of night air
the cool moss embraces us.
We are drenched in a hoop of light,
a constellation of fireflies.

Margaret Speak

Romantic Notions

He down one end of the phone
she down the other on her bed.
They are talking about what it means to love.

And she can sense him
from his darkness moving out
to believe that love between two people can grow.

But all the while she is sceptical
that there is such a thing
as that core of flowering:

a romantic notion
that, yes, secretly she longs for
but has long ago told herself does not exist.

What about the day by day loving?
She thinks about her father,
his handling of plants.

His chunky fingers
separating root from root
oozed such feeling and kindness

patience and giving
that the plant
when placed in the soil, could only grow.

Sarah Boyes

Do You Like Chocolate?

What you'll think about faithfulness,
or peace at any price, I know;
but not if you like chocolate.

I see, in the quiet of late afternoon
how your breasts, brown as an egg,
cast a lavender shadow as you turn,

not making me wait, while light
slips between the curtains
and hands and mouth create

our speechless language, inflected
with sweat and sighs. Dozing,
joined at hip and thigh,

I'm suddenly pierced awake, wanting
all you ever knew of bus stops in the rain
and washing up, the string your life

is threaded on. Pain, domestic beast,
unthreatening as a hearthrug,
climbs on our bed and lies beside us.

I can't know your shopping list
of days. Always, that long word's
already out of date.

Your hands, full of wild honey,
are rueful on the sting.
Look. Here's our own shortlist.

Do you like chocolate?

Kate Foley

How

is it possible to know another's love?
I only know my own, I cannot melt
into you, I cannot become you: my legs will
never be yours, although the flat of my hand knows
how the hairs on your thigh

stand up under it, like grass just before it goes
spiky in July, half-scratching the tender middle
of my palm, and my fingertips know
how soft is the skin between your shoulder blades,
warm and smooth as kid-leather gloves,

but it is not my skin although
sometimes the weight of your hands holding my wrists
on the pillow above me just before your fingers
lace through mine like weeds
is so familiar, the lines on your palms as they run

over my forearms press maps into my flesh,
and your face is as only I will ever see it, and so close
to mine I almost forget that you are
over me, that you are not me, that what I see
is more than a reflection.

Barbara Marsh

Sometimes in the morning

Sometimes in the morning,
before mouth noise chase away knowing,
sea murmur sweetness against rock,
whispering loud to interpret dreams.
One morning like that,
sea roll into my dreams like is sea know the meaning.
And sea murmuring,
Think how man flow here without clothes, without nothing,
think how woman swim in with not one stitch to she name.
Woman that come with nothing, going out without one thing.
Sea nibbling murmurs against rock,
then mouth erupt and you can't tell what was dream, what was wake.
Is shouting and slapping between rock and sea,
and it hard to remember the murmuring that happen
in the rock-whispering morning.

Merle Collins

With You

I stand with you in the garden
The birds' surprising madrigals
Rise through the roar of bees.

I stand with you in the kitchen
Dear damaged long loved over used
Pans and pots protect us.

I stand with you in the hallway
With the deep oak tick of the clock
And the turning stair.

We sit by books in the lamplight
Importunate nondescript dog and cat
Surround us warmly.

We lie in the lofty bedroom
The church clock through the window
Quartering Gloucestershire silences.

Without you, no garden.
Sunshine withers on the plum tree
House shrinks derelict into dust.

R V Bailey

Atlas

There is a kind of love called maintenance,
Which stores the WD40 and knows when to use it;

Which checks the insurance, and doesn't forget
The milkman; which remembers to plant bulbs;

Which answers letters; which knows the way
The money goes; which deals with dentists

And Road Fund Tax and meeting trains,
And postcards to the lonely; which upholds

The permanently ricketty elaborate
Structures of living; which is Atlas.

And maintenance is the sensible side of love,
Which knows what time and weather are doing
To my brickwork; insulates my faulty wiring;
Laughs at my dryrotten jokes; remembers
My need for gloss and grouting; which keeps
My suspect edifice upright in air,
As Atlas did the sky.

U A Fanthorpe

The Orpheus Variation

Who'd believe, meeting us now,
that once we saw daylight undress each other

our skin smooth and cool as tiles:
that our breath stirred the leaves

in each other's hair?

Fiona Sampson

Mistress Raven

Why do I weep for Mistress Raven
torn wings folded along her back?
We used to dance the wild fandango
fingers going click click, click clack.

Why do I weep for Mistress Raven
is it the fuse of her almond eyes?
Her smiling mouth red as arousal
but whose the flattery, whose the lies?

Why do I weep for Mistress Raven
cold tears streaming on my cheek?
Do I long for the grip of claws?
Do I dream of the tap of a beak?

Why do I weep for Mistress Raven?
The world ignites at the tap of her shoe.
My feathers are burnt in the gold of your fire,
quoth the bird, who sits on the smouldering yew.

Why do I weep for Mistress Raven
is she the mirror of my soul?
Then cover the glass with her long black hair
for my secret desires must never be told.

Why do I weep for Mistress Raven
torn wings folded along her back?
We used to dance the wild fandango
fingers going click click, click clack.

Berta Freistadt

Hunger

She is thinking of the last time he touched her –
how he stroked her, said she was losing weight

as if it represented a country they had to get to, as if
the fat could curl back to the bone like years undone.

And she saw they stood between their shadows and the wolf
who howls for them in the night.

Katherine Gallagher

The Rigger's Wife

His unaccustomed weight left bruises tattoo-blue
against her skin; he'd said
she was thinner, touching the veins
that ran hyacinth ribbons
under her wrist. His muscles, sinews
now were hard and strong as hawsers.
Watching the early light defining his sleeping shape,
she slowly relearned the familiar lines
of this wedded stranger,
this rare visitor come to her bed.

And lay wondering:
what now of her fragile, defensive structures,
the patterns she'd woven for living alone?
Her life-lines would catch him like cobwebs,
he'd toss and struggle
tearing, by accident
or design, his own ropes
flowing out of him
coil on coil; snaring her
with his leashes, plaits
of silk and steel.

In time they'd mesh again,
make the net of love to swing inside.
Until the appointed day when
he'd up and go – and she left hanging.

A breathing space
a sense of floating:
before she picked up the threads.

Rose Flint

Divorce

I must begin to scrape away
The bloody black sediment of years
The crackle and spit of words,
Insult and many tears and pain.
The longing to be clean again.

I start to cry.
But stop to hear his quiet reply
And when he speaks
He speaks from his heart
"We tear each other apart" you say
"Not just once but every day".

S. Fairclough

Formerly

Staying in the former wife's wing
of my very own former Scottish home
with you, my former English husband,
the father of my transatlantic children
is easy, since I know where everything is.
I can find the bathroom in the dark
and I know where the light switch is.
The china pattern pleases me as much
as it did the day I picked it out.
The pillows and quilts are tasteful too,
though I don't like the boot rack at all.
It's crammed with walking shoes and socks
I've never seen and dainty boots for hiking.
Correction. This is your former *wives'* wing.

Linda Chase

A Compression of Distances

The roof bosses of Winchester Cathedral on our 20th wedding anniversary

We could, I said, hold
one in our hands: trace
how the stone leaves
are entwined like held

hands. And then, you said,
see how the boss holds
the roof's ribs of stone, how the lines
gather speed.

Like the early universe, I said,
moving faster and faster
towards light years.
The geometry of space

and the curving of galaxies.
Then think about our space,
you said, and the curve of our bodies
together. Suddenly

our anthem, Mozart's *Ave verum,*
rose through the stone spaces
compressing time
and distance. Intersections

of stone and time held us.
Think of the word games we've shared,
all the stories you've told me, the rich ways
of our life... Look how each knot

of stone is an ease and complexity of leaves.

Daphne Gloag

Not exactly a David

You stood in welcome, arms outstretched,
muscled as he was, skin darkened to teak
by years of wind, lacking only patina
from crowds stroking your thighs, feeling
for imperfections in the stone.

You'd weathered well, I thought: scarcely
an ounce of excess fat, still firm
just where you should be. My fingers sensed
no sagging in your flesh, no paper skin,
no ridging blood vessels. I felt

your heartbeat next to mine, could hear
your breathing find my rhythm, knew
for sure you were no statue. We stood
almost unmoving, let heat run through us,
warming our armature of aging bone.

Lyn Moir

Voyage

I lie on the narrow bed, you in my arms;
this is our last night, love, but you are tired.
My mind drifts to another time, your eyes
sea-blue above the old steel-string guitar
we used to sing to. Then to your hands'
first rippling touch, my 'wild surmise'!
How we lay coiled upon a single bed
or cavorted across its sturdy frame
like sailors running the spinnaker.
Now we rest, becalmed in the slow swell
of your heaving chest. Beneath the instruments
that chart your path, we sleep. I dream of you
holding me in our little craft, and wake
when your arm falls from me, knowing you've gone.

Jill Sharp

145

The Widow's Mite: Effie, Dumfries, August 1916

Bring out the boots that will no longer need to be repaired.

Bring them to the bare hillside.

Lovely is the harebell.
Still, frail.

I will take up my anger like a torn floorboard,
a bed.

'Thy will be done.' I said.

Dust of the August afternoon is everywhere.

Dust motes.

I'll gather all the holes together here.

Gillian Allnutt

Last Wish

Before I go down to the ferryman
All set for the final journey
I'll find me a Cork or Kerry man
From Droom or Ballyvourney

He'll be lean as an Irish wolfhound
With eyes of emerald green
Rugged as Boggaragh Mountains
Salty as Skibbereen

Smooth as a pint of Guinness
He'll flatter in fluent blarney
He'll kiss me with his leprechaun lips
From Dingle to Killarney

To the saucy skip of his fiddle
I'll be dancing till I'm giddy
He'll set my feet a-jigging from
Kishneam to Ringaskiddy

And when I need to rest my legs
He'll pour the best poteen
Distilled by a Catholic brother
By the road to Carrigaline

He'll whisper tales in the old tongue
To make me tired and teary
Feeding the fire with turves of peat
From Sneem and Ballymakeery

I long to be wild and feckless once
Before the final tally
Lord, send me a Cork or Kerry man
From Crookstown or Stradbally

And over the bright green hills we'll dance
And over the golden sands
With the soft mist in our eyes, Lord,
And a shamrock in our hands

Elisabeth Rowe

Part 6

Relationships

Full Moon with My Grandmother

Because your time is short, we draw it out,
like this early summer evening by the sea,
as we prolong our talk, delay the hour I leave,
though now the pier is lit with electric light,
or a winter midnight, when we stood and stared
at the full moon on the water, like a path
to the other side of life. I wanted to ask,
'Where will it take you? Will I see you there?'
The stars above are already burnt and gone
by the time we spy them, which goes to prove
a memory of dust and ashes lingers on,
and if we choose to, we may call this love.
As you sail alone to another shore, know
my footsteps in the sand are here. I follow.

Sarah Wardle

1

Growing a Girl

At her hand I learned to feast –
platefuls of bacon and glistening eggs,
tinned tomatoes pooled in bowls,
King Edwards big as babies' heads
borne from the cave-cold cellar.
I got everything down my neck
as if she were fattening me up for winter.

As a growing girl she'd known slaughter –
her father torn to pieces at the Somme,
her mother nourishing grievance ever after
feeding on the best at breakfast, dinner, tea,
sucking the sweet flesh of the Easter lamb,
hooking out the marrow with a skewer
until her face shone with grease.

Gran had iron in her hungry blood.
She remembered all the old cuts –
brisket, oxtail, trotters, tripe,
liver, kidney, heart, tongue.
She prepared those dark and savoury meats
with knowledge culled from grief and war:
she skinned a rabbit when she put me to sleep.

Esther Morgan

Mute

Little tree as empty as a house
when your mother is not at home,
few or yellow or promising
they will come back, your syllables
are loose circles blown about
barely forming words, your leaves
amount to nothing without her saying
*You look lovely standing there
in your hair and your dress.*

Martha Kapos

Bluebells

I wasn't very old when my father came
and took me out from boarding school
to tell me my mother was dead.
She had left him for another man,
then got ill. She wasn't happy
at the end. It was May.
We parked the car by a Devon wood
and picked a big bunch of bluebells
for her grave.
I didn't go to the funeral.
Now when I see bluebells under trees
with their sappy stems bowing
from their freight of bells
pealing a subtler scent
than their chunkier hyacinth cousins;
or when I see them in a vase,
how unhappy they are when cut,
how fast they fade,
I feel a pain in my heart.
I remember how pretty and gay she was,
the stories I heard of her courage
when we were babies in wartime Japan
(getting home to England in '42),
how effusive and ready to laugh or cry,
how they complemented, loved each other
and warmed us till things went wrong,
when she wept more and more –
'Oh, don't! Don't!' – and then died young.
Earth to earth but for me each May
she and the new bluebells are inseparable.

Dinah Livingstone

from: Mother

Silences
between us like
black owls asleep,

we smile
across quiet talons,
feather on feather
trapping soft darkness.

Images of blood
and tearing
make us fear to wake
these birds
that eat our light.

They hunt in dreams.

If I could speak,
I would ask
why there is always a child
crying in my head.

I remember my father's
whip of words,
but you are nebulous,
bright but insubstantial;

I needed you solid as bread.

Isobel Thrilling

Glove

I check the wardrobe one last time.
A red leather glove clawing its way out.
Escapee from yesterday's black bags.
I smooth it. Tiny holes like pores.
She wore this pair on sports day.
Striding across the playing field
between clumps of teenagers
in that dress of huge poppies,
and a straw hat. Didn't she know
it was nineteen sixty five
and Christine White listening to
Ticket To Ride on her tranny behind me?

Straw hat, red gloves and a white handbag
swinging from her elbow as she waved
and I cringed.

I measure the glove against my hand.
Mine is tiny.
Heats, medals, cups, county,
regional, and finally, national level,
all to come. And she was there.
Big, red hands sweeping canteens,
hoovering offices. So I could run.

Marilyn Ricci

Handnotes

My mother hated gesturing. My speech
was always reinforced by hands, made concrete
by the shapes I drew in air.

So mother found my talk embarrassing,
her Puritan ancestors stronger than she knew,
no mother of her own to play the fingergames
small children use to reinforce
the wordspace time eventually fills.

But when I'd grown, and matched my growing with
a lexical increase, my fingers too
grew fluent, so a sort of doublespeak
emerged, language complete with detailed handnotes.

"Frills," mother would scoff. Seeing her real discomfort,
I would try mental straitjacketing, arms tight to sides.
Five minutes, max, and then, wild animals constrained
by sheltering, they'd twitch, too curious for caution.

It would be good to take my mother's hand again
and talk, get down to feelings once too near the bone.

Lyn Moir

from Year: May

After an hour, two hours
in the garden,
after I've scrubbed my hands
with soap and a nailbrush
and after the damp
from the cleaning has dried,

I rub them together,
stroke fingers, backs of fingers;
they're not like my hands,
but like my Mam's
after a shift stoking the boiler
at Eastgate;
stacking tables.

Where do I begin
to tell you how right this feels?
That on the dry knuckles
of each index finger
there is a history of skin
that both is and is not my own.

Jacqueline Gabbitas

My Mother's Perfume

Strange how her perfume used to arrive long before she did,
    a jade cloud that sent me hurrying
first to the loo, then to an upstairs window to watch for her taxi.
    I'd prepare myself
by trying to remember her face, without feeling afraid. As she drew
    nearer I'd get braver
until her scent got so strong I could taste the coins in the bottom
    of her handbag.
And here I am forty years on, still half-expecting her. Though now
    I just have to open
the stopper of an expensive French bottle, daring only a whiff of
    Shalimar
which Jacques Guerlain created from the vanilla orchid vine.
    Her ghostly face
might shiver like Christ's on Veronica's veil – a green-gold blossom
    that sends me back
to the first day of the school holidays, the way I used to practise
    kissing her cheek
by kissing the glass. My eyes scanned the long road for a speck
    while the air turned amber.
Even now, the scent of vanilla stings like a cane. But I can also smell
    roses and jasmine
in the bottle's top notes, my legs wading through the fragrant path,
    to the gloved hand emerging
from a black taxi at the gate of Grandmother's garden. And for a
    moment I think I am safe.
Then Maman turns to me with a smile like a dropped
    perfume bottle, her essence spilt.

Pascale Petit

156

Flood: IV

For you, I'm breaking fifty years of silence
before my death reseals the past for good.

Once, my mother was too ill
to queue for soup – nothing but knobs of gristle
in greasy water. I knew the lack
would be enough to tip her under.
I tried to give her mine; she wouldn't take it.
"You're young and strong, your chance is best."
The wooden bowl jigged back and forth –
like two English gentlemen in a doorway!
In the end we shared it. We took turns
feeding spoonfuls to each other.

Remember this, for the tide is rising again.
When you're coffled by hunger and terror,
packed in too closely for big gestures,
you have to take the little opportunities:
wash your face; look at a leaf;
give away one spoonful of your soup.
Else you are conniving in the murder.

Believe me, I know, for I was there
and every single night I'm there again.

Stevie Krayer

Still Light

You picture your mother as a tree
– somehow that makes it easier.
A silver birch, undressing
unhurriedly, as though days were years,
while a fine rain plays
like jazz in her hair. She drops
her fine, white leaves
one by one. Her branches
are almost bare now. See,
how beautiful she is against the darkening sky.

Shazea Quraishi

Grapes

No remaining leaves, just bunches of grapes
against the wall, naked and blue; some glossy,
others mildewed, white and seemingly frosty,
but fine despite the blemishes and odd shapes.

And later, working where the bank tapers,
I find the fruits of the viburnum lost
among dead leaves, hidden in spreading moss,
like tiny eyes surprised to see me there.

Large and heavy, vessel of six offspring,
each night her undressed body amazes me.
Scarred with the history a long life brings,

she's small and simple, soft and ordinary;
in feeling, thinking, acting and believing
so complex and extraordinary.

Lucy Hamilton

The Night My Father Died

The night he died, I took my mother to swim.
We slipped our bodies naked,
into the lunar-coloured lake and gasped.

Her body became strong and she swam
as if she had just been born.
I watched her bobbing shoulders,
halves of a pale shell.

She moved towards me and our fingers touched.
I understood then that we were crying.

Rebecca Goss

Distances

I see my mother waving – her unfussed, smiling
au revoir, alone on her verandah,
a small figure half-covered by shadow.

I hold her wave, see myself sharing it
eightfold, once for each of us – a wave
we have grown into

as she perfected it, voiced it over years
listening for the two who died,
losses she carried into her skin,
her children
the only trophies she ever wanted.

Now I search her face
contained, real as light,
hear over her words sewn into
the wave, 'There are many kinds of love
and I have lived some of them'.

Katherine Gallagher

Stepmother

She was very small,
she always wore black,
she was not in mourning
for her life or anybody else's.
And I loved her.

Straight of back, elegant of foot,
a tiny wild cat fearing nothing;
offering the startled burglar a cup of tea,
though white hot Irish temper flared
alarmingly at cruel words or deeds.

She was a champion of pitiful things –
bones begged from the butcher
for a one-eyed, mangy mutt,
smelly sprats boiled up for the alley cat,
and the child that was me rescued

from festering boredom in a cold city –
shown a world undreamed of:
London seen through pillars of white,
lime juice and cheese straws to eat,
a soft divan to sleep on.

Most mornings, even now, fifty years on
I wake expecting her for breakfast:
coffee, croissants, cherry jam –
till I remember with a tiny pang
she left me years ago.

Eve Pearce

Cling Film

She saves up used cling film for me.
I've never worked out why.

I've watched how she spreads a piece out
with the flat of her hands, smoothing it over

and over again, muttering, as if trying
to straighten things out (something

between us?) There are still tell-tale wrinkles.
This once drum-tight skin can never be virgin,

no matter how much she tries to stretch it.
Don't get me wrong – it's always clean.

My mother-in-law's a stickler for hygiene.
Her house smells of *Steradent*, *Omo* and moth balls.

Lorna Dowell

Lena, our maid

She anchored all my needs
In her solidity,
A cross pleat on her brow.

Between her household chores
She'd rush with me to school,
Her square hands rough with love.

Devout, she made me kneel
On crowded pavement slabs
To watch the bishop pass

Under his baldachin
Intoning Latin chant,
The incense cloud above.

At the stone kitchen sink,
Her yeasty body's shrine,
She'd stand and strip-wash clean,

Then outings into town
To dark room secrecy
Where she collected hope

From a clairvoyant's words
Behind a curtain fall,
Her love-life's counterpoint.

A butcher boy appeared
And many nights they sighed
On mother's lounge settee

While I pretended sleep
Two doors away. She got
Her man and left. I cried.

Her home two basement rooms
Where she would lie in wait
With plates of chips, the food

I loved, spoiling my lunch.
But still I hear her screams
Up in my room, two floors

Above her flat, when she
Gave birth to her huge son,
Her second child, she said.

Lotte Kramer

Dear Evelyn,

I couldn't have managed without you,
without the rides I used to have on your back,
the sense of moving forward;
your win on the pools glittered

on your horizon; you were moving towards it
on your kneeling mat, polishing our floor;
it was somewhere in the white skirting boards
or was it in the garden among the forget-me-nots

when we spat on stale bread for luck,
took it to feed the ducks; and you taught me
to pour tea into my saucer to cool
the times I was late for the bus, then slurp it up?

When I win, you said, *I'll buy you
a satin dress, I'll take you to Butlins*,
and I knew you would, somewhere
on the fairground where you could play bingo
for a huge shiny doll or a goldfish,

I'll win you one with ping-pong balls, our lass.

Pam Zinnemann-Hope

Mrs Haywood

She scrubbed at floors (my mother's), pushed her straggling hair,
Shuffled her rough knees, intent on mud,
Rubbed, at each worn brick. I would never be
Like her – no, not poor, but so intent
She forgot the knobbled body.

Can worlds of roots, high world of air
Touch this life? Now I raise, trembling,
The brown, brimmed bowl. She was almost there.

Alison Brackenbury

162

Women's Medical

Without the wig
a fuzz of white hair,
grey-pink skull.

In for a few tests
I tried to avoid
her jawbone,
the cracked bell
of her rib cage.

One lung gone,
the other suspect,
her muted cough
punctuated our sleep.

We waited for my results.
'Negative' I told her.
'Home tomorrow.'

She asked to wash my hair.
I couldn't refuse,
helped her
open the bottle,
turn the stiff tap
fill the sink.

My head in her lap,
the rough hospital towel
scratching my face
as she softly rubbed
my thick mane dry.

Patricia Pogson

2

Mother and Daughter

She rides the wind
like a kite pulling taut
against the mooring
of my restraining hand.
When a sudden gust
jerks the string
the frantic head
dips and veers
this way and that
desperate to break the thread,
soar up out of sight.
I, grounded today,
cup my hand to shield
the small flame of myself.

Anne Grimes

Graffiti

Woken at midnight, I follow arrows
like a childhood game towards Casualty
to find you here in this bleak cubicle.

Sixteen, still in your party gear, all black –
stockings, shirt and scarf, your
grandmother's jet beads, a tattered shadow
sprawled against these cracked white tiles
where someone has sprayed
Fuck the Bastards,

I stretch out a hand to touch you, to lift
the hair back from your smeared cheeks,
back from the vomit-crusted O
of your mouth, but you push me away,
black tears, scrawled
across the white wall of your face,
the only message you have for me.

Angela Kirby

Outgrown
for Zoe

It is both sad and a relief to fold so carefully
her outgrown clothes and line up the little worn shoes
of childhood, so prudent, scuffed and particular.
It is both happy and horrible to send them galloping
back tappity-tap along the misty chill path into the past.

It is both a freedom and a prison, to be outgrown
by her as she towers over me as thin as a sequin
in her doc martens and her pretty skirt,
because just as I work out how to be a mother
she stops being a child.

Penelope Shuttle

Black Shells

I found them washed up
at the foot of your bed
after you'd gone;
laceless, gaping, ankle-boots,
discarded like two black shells.

Fingering the soft hollows,
the indents of your toes
I know your whole world is weighted here.
The gospel of your life.
I can still feel your first kick,
the quickening.

But you have outworn
these black boots –
are making new impressions now.
Perhaps tomorrow I will wrap them
in paper and place them with
your doll's crib, your tea-set, your books.

Denise Bennett

When The Waters Break

On your sixtieth
a daughter sings *happy birthday*
down the phone.

Looking at the 5 a.m. digital
you aren't surprised
when the call ends abruptly

and she screams *Not many more now*.
When her acute phase
has passed you accept the diagnosis

of schizophrenia, and drink
bottle after bottle of cheap
red wine, but in the dawn

when once your waters broke
words hand you back an emptiness
it's difficult to grieve for.

Wendy French

Because you do not come to me in days

Because you do not come to me in days
you come to me in dreams.
You wait in hallways
saying that your money's all been stolen
so you have to go to the Riviera.
What can this mean?
I wait for night,
a supplicant on the temple steps
shaded by gingkos. I wait for night,
for darkness, for the young avatar to come out,
the one who knows everything,
who knows about repair
and pity. Who brings a glimpse of you to me
for pity, in the night.

Julia Casterton

Bridal

Learning elegance in the drape and fall
of duchess satin, splendour in being tall,
you turn in front of the wide mirror. Slip
a hand over white bodice, white-contoured hip.
Miraculous as the moment you were born –
three weeks too soon – slippery and quick
in a cream robe of lanolin, from slicked head
to purple toes. The midwife smiled and said
how rare it was, the best, most precious
emollient in the world as she smoothed just
a little on my cheek and placed you
muslin-muffled at my breast, brand-new.
We drank our future together, blessed,
my thumb inside one tiny seeking fist.

Sally Carr

3

My Sister Lets Down Her Hair

into the winter bedroom and I turn
to the hollow of the bed we share,
her warmth still there and her smell.

It is coming on seven and she moves
by touch to her dressing. I know
every move of her and follow
her every move by the lamp of her golden hair.
As it was yesterday, and the day before,
so shall it be now in memory
a prayer for her going forth.

                             Back then
we are lit in the cold morning by only
her rivery hair, the strong flow of her hair,
in the mirror her golden hair. The little
clouds of our breath eddy across the room
to the further shore of the window
giving on gardens and sheds. She keeps
an eye for the factory bus. Its lights
probing the room at last, she'll pick
up her bag and go from the house
without disturbing a soul.

I shift into her spot in the bed, an animal's lair,
lined with dreams and the smell of her hair,
till the dawn comes up with its clear, or its cloudy, light
wishing her back to haunt the day
with her rivery hair, her golden hair,
and I am any creature left for lonely.

Paula Meehan

Pictures Against Skin

Something in this room. We knew the place
by heart – that never mattered:
sisters following the space from blade
to blade, spiralling round
the nodules of the spine
and up again – a careful phrasing
ended at the full stop of the nape.
Feeling the muscles wriggle, skin
curl up with pleasure
prolonged by guessing wrongly: mirror, vase . . .

They are still here, so many of her things,
the blemished glass, the china
velvety with dust along the sill.
Drawn separately to this room
after the service, we meet
around the massive centrepiece –
not our grandmother's bed, but ours,
thrusting the past insistently
between us. The highlight of each visit:
to sleep all three together, tucked

beneath the perfumed camouflage
of eiderdowns, sliding down,
our spirits soon subsiding
into hushed intent – the games devised
to bridge the chasm yawning
before sleep.
Fingers delicately drawing in the dark
translated into pictures passed
from back to back
our speechless happiness at being here.

I have let slip the memory, and laugh,
and wonder, too,
which of us is ever touched in that way
now, with such tenderness.
And in a rare apologetic movement
we lean across the faded quilt,
lips grazing lips, a cheek, searching beneath
the scent we choose to wear to funerals
a trace of that familiarity,
the odour of another, younger skin.

Caroline Price

The First Cut

In the womb we sucked each other's thumb. As toddlers we curled together like kittens and rubbed each other's earlobes. Thirteen years later, she sits in front of me dressed in a hospital gown. Her body is still that of a child, and her hair, which has never been cut, is braided into one long plait and draped over her shoulder. Her emaciated arms are discoloured by lesions. "You brought the scissors?" She extends her palm with a cold solemnity. I hand over the scissors and hold taut the tail of her plait while she cuts, cuts, cuts thickly at its base, close beside her neck. I am stunned by its weight when it falls into my lap. There it lies, measuring the distance that has always been between us.

Helen Pizzey

I am hers and she is mine

When I was young I knitted flocks of sheep.
I kept them like an army on the landing,
drilled to watch her door, and storm her room,
reporting back on everything they saw.
And in the winter as the days drew in
I knitted every sheep a little cardigan
to keep them warm at night while they waited.
They waited. But she never came back.
She went away to be a grown woman.
Our partnership however gathered strength.
We spent our lives perfecting being enemies
and now it's automatic: I am hers
and she – whom now I only meet in dreams,
with painted face and dogs on chains – is mine.

Selima Hill

Morning Sickness

For my sister

I am riding the backwash
of your feelings – your exhaustion
is mine, the sickening swings
through elation, fear. My breasts
are tender with your heavy
tenderness; I tread gently,
examine my own urine for signs
of your bleeding. And find myself
buying tinned fruit, or nursing
a custard pudding, steeling myself
to sink the spoon into its pale
pocked flesh. I hold my breath
as you count the days to that second
pulse, that proof of life – certain
I have it already, jumping
beneath my ribs. Heart to heart,
we travel together for twelve
full weeks; and then the road
splits – your hand slips from mine,
and I watch your back moving
steadily into the future; leaving me
in this place, this cul de sac
where all my attempts to follow
dissolve, their unresolved shreds
left like a tidemark round me.

Caroline Price

The Labour Room

I may have thought how strange it was
that the sister I used to balance
on hands and feet for acrobatic shows
in the lounge, the little girl

who used to dance on the wide ledge
of the bedroom window with next door's boys,
was now spread out on this trestle
her swollen sex every shade of maroon.

But when the flamboyant red parted
like a vertical lid and the blind white crown
of my niece appeared, when she lay
between my sister's slack knees,
bluish and floury, her cry as mundane
and miraculous as you could wish,

and when I watched the midwife draw down
the perfect lobes of the placenta
with its marbled cord, exotic as a waterlily,
for that moment I understood everything
and the world hung ripe in my reach.

Sue Rose

4

Ghosts

The ghosts that haunt us are an ill-matched pair.
Our old selves at thirteen could not have known
this friendship. I would have thought you posh.
You would have thought me common. Close touch
unravels years, uncovering lost tracks.

When you were thirteen your mother sent you
away from her to school, to misery,
hundreds of miles. I see you pale and proud,
your high brainy forehead, your veiled eyes
denying the tremor of your mouth, obedient.

When I was thirteen already masking
pain in hair dye, lipstick, sulky silence,
my mother went away from me, taking
all warmth and colour. She left me nightmares,
a head full of whispers, missing, missing.

Skin to skin we conjured up these girls,
still hopelessly thirteen despite the years.
Accusing. Yours feels I pack her off,
mine that you dump her. We'll introduce them.
They can argue, blame their mothers. We'll
slip away together, find a different track.

Cynthia Fuller

Grey Sweater
in memoriam Helen Richards

From all the elegant clothes you left behind
I chose just one : a sweater soft as goose down,
as easy on my back
as sunshine on fells
cropped by sheep.
The colour of clouds sweeping over hills,
it smelt of clover and trodden grass,
of sharp north winds, harbingers of snow.

That was twenty years ago:
today I pull it from the drawer,
slip it over my head,
hear children's laughter
as I flick chalk from the sleeve.

Elizabeth Rapp

The Whole World

Was it the worst song ever? A silly lie?

School-girls used to sing it on school outings,
to hum it, the folksy nonsense of our time,

*'He has the whole world in his hands. He has the whole
wide world in his hands ...'*

Something like that.

Maxine, when I learnt you'd died, I came straight here –
the ocean rim and white September sky
locked round me like a helmet, like a tough phone-call,

'What happens when I die, will I have peace?'

I always offered, *'Live for the day!'* –
Each time I wrote, you rang,

'Sorry I haven't replied.'   'No need.'

Phone-calls were tender. We never tried harder,
not sitting Tripos – and, while we spoke,
we laid an ear to the ground,
we held a tumbler to the party-wall.

My turn to ask a question:

*'Is there enough life for you here –
do you feel it, even in its ravaged state?'*

The world is torn up at my feet; the waves darken
with an undertow of scavanged weed.

I think of living acres of red dulse;
fronds sway about, reaching out for swimmers
with thousands of tiny, blood-stained arms.

Empty mussel-shells – loving pairs still hinged
with sticky, extruded filiaments,
their colour an intense emotional blue –
cast up on shore and knock on pebbles.

I see thick-glued, tall banks of breathing mussels,
the colour of school summer-dresses,
and, sibilant as choirs of girls, the bi-valves sing,

'In his hands. He has the whole world in his hands ...'

I dreamt last night. My dream concerned letters –
those I wrote and those you said gave comfort.

A stack sat on the post-box: flames billowed,
curved directly from the post-box red;
fire never touched, but the pages melted.

I can't recall a word of my letters.

You said the same about your patients:

'Vanished', you said, when you became so ill,
*'No thoughts of much-loved patients now –
my whole world gone!'*

Not *'He'*, we find *'Him'* easy to reject,
not *'in his hands'*, unless a butterfingers,
distracted God who let you slip –

but *'whole'*, *'the whole world'* ... I think
we make the world, and worlds may be re-made.

Dilys Wood

The Hare
i.m. Frances Horovitz 1938–1983

That March night I remember how we heard
a baby crying in a neighbouring room
but found him sleeping quietly in his cot.

The others went to bed and we sat late
talking of children and the men we loved.
You thought you'd like another child. 'Too late'

you said. And we fell silent, thought a while
of yours with his copper hair and mine,
a grown daughter and sons.

Then, that joke we shared, our phases of the moon.
'Sisterly lunacy' I said. You liked
the phrase. It became ours. Different

as earth and air, yet in one trace that week
we towed the calends like boats reining
the oceans of the world at the full moon.

Suddenly from the fields we heard again
a baby cry, and standing at the door
listened for minutes, eyes and ears soon used

to the night. It was cold. In the east
the river made a breath of shining sound.
The cattle in the field were shadow black.

A cow coughed. Some slept, and some pulled grass.
I could smell blossom from the blackthorn
and see their thorny crowns against the sky.

And then again, a sharp cry from the hill.
'A hare' we said together, not speaking
of fox or trap that held it in a lock

of terrible darkness. Both admitted
next day to lying guilty hours awake
at the crying of the hare. You told me

of sleeping at last in the jaws of a bad dream.
'I saw all the suffering of the world
in a single moment. Then I heard

a voice say "But this is nothing, nothing
to the mental pain." ' I couldn't speak of it.
I thought about your dream as you lay ill.

In the last heavy nights before full moon,
when its face seems sorrowful and broken,
I look through binoculars. Its seas flower

like cloud over water, it wears its craters
like silver rings. Even in dying you
menstruated as a woman in health

considering to have a child or no.
When they hand me insults or little hurts
and I'm on fire with my arguments

at your great distance you can calm me still.
Your dream, my sleeplessness, the cattle
asleep under a full moon,

and out there
the dumb and stiffening body of the hare.

Gillian Clarke

For Mimi's Birthday: Alcaics

Dear, how I hate the overblown diction of
lines for occasions: festschrifts, like elegies
    making a banal birthday seem to
     signpost a passage to unmapped wasteland,

when thoughts and smiles are fresh as they've ever been –
at least my brief years given the privilege
    of bantering across some table,
     words made more fluent by cakes or curries

or by the short time left for exchanging them:
train in an hour, expresso in Styrofoam
    cups. Ciao! I wish ... I'll tell you next time.
     Bus to the Eurostar, airport taxi.

I'll never see the light of your memories
(joy can be shared, but losses are separate)
    though we're a lucky pair of outcasts,
     free to embellish or keep our stories.

177

Yours, Mimi, silver's brilliance on velvety
shapes in the no-man's land between alphabets
　　you were obliged to cross and cross to
　　write in the white ink of exiled childhood.

Whose children *did* we talk about, smoking and
sipping red wine (an Indian family
　　toasting some milestone near us) in the
　　restaurant tucked behind Euston station?

Two women, poised for middle-aged liberty,
still have our fledgling burdens to anchor us,
　　wish they were soaring, independent,
　　glad when they ground us with tea and gossip.

Think of friendships lost to geography,
or lost to language, sex, or its absence ... I
　　send, crossing fingers, crossing water,
　　bright thoughts, bright Maryam: happy birthday.

Marilyn Hacker

Note: alcaics are an iambic verse form (named after Alcaeus of Lesbos, 6th century BC) much used by Horace in the 'Odes' and may consist of a four line stanza with two eleven syllable lines, one of nine syllables and one of twelve.

Tact

I dozed off on the dunes
and my bag was open,
sun-warmed sand clinging
to comb, return ticket, keys.

My friend came from nowhere
as they do in dreams,
and said I was snoring –
said it kindly, with tact.

For years we had talked
about the trivial and profound
but never seen each other asleep.
It was an intrusion

among tufts of grass on the dunes.
Later she rang
and I told my dream
without resentment.

A slight pause
and the soft explosion
of that intimate laugh,
just for the two of us.

Beata Duncan

Warming Her Pearls
for Judith Radstone

Next to my own skin, her pearls. My mistress
bids me wear them, warm them, until evening
when I'll brush her hair. At six, I place them
round her cool, white throat. All day I think of her,

resting in the Yellow Room, contemplating silk
or taffeta, which gown tonight? She fans herself
whilst I work willingly, my slow heat entering
each pearl. Slack on my neck, her rope.

She's beautiful. I dream about her
in my attic bed; picture her dancing
with tall men, puzzled by my faint, persistent scent
beneath her French perfume, her milky stones.

I dust her shoulders with a rabbit's foot,
watch the soft blush seep through her skin
like an indolent sigh. In her looking-glass
my red lips part as though I want to speak.

Full moon. Her carriage brings her home. I see
her every movement in my head... Undressing,
taking off her jewels, her slim hand reaching
for the case, slipping naked into bed, the way

she always does... And I lie here awake,
knowing the pearls are cooling even now
in the room where my mistress sleeps. All night
I feel their absence and I burn.

Carol Ann Duffy

179

The Black Chair

Now I am inside the room
after all the dreaded waiting;
a woman is kinder, more gentle.

So you have me open my mouth;
I open it gladly for you.
Tiny mirrors, softly you tell

your assistant the language of ivory:
my vowels, my consonants, my country.
It is all unfathomable to me

but it sounds beautiful, rhythmical.
I could be crumbling, spotted with decay;
maybe need a filling, a cap, root canal.

My abscess is a mystery, a swollen book.
You tuck me up and put me to sleep.
My soft swollen gums are stroked, all red,

my tiny dark holes prodded
by one of your strange foreign instruments.
They lie at my side now, gleaming

sharp as a family, smiling in a silver album.
I am laid back on your director's chair –
the pink glass of champagne at my side.

Every so often I rise for a moment
like a woman rising from a dream of the dead
like a woman standing up on a horse

to drink and swirl and spit and watch
my own frothy blood spin and disappear.
You say good, good, you're doing fine,

again, again, till your voice is a love song
and every cavity an excuse for meeting;
floss is the long length of string

that keeps us parted. My mouth is parted.
You are in it with your white gloved hands
I have not eaten garlic for weeks.

But you don't need to pull any teeth
alas, no molars to come out in your hands
no long roots, no spongy bits of gum.

We won't go that far. No. It's surface stuff
really. Not nearly as deep as you or I could go.
You'll polish them. You'll give the odd amalgam.

You'll x-ray. You'll show me the photo.
I'll look at my own teeth on the white screen.
They tell me nothing about myself.

My teeth, speechless.
Rootless pearls, anonymous white things.
I need you to tell me about myself.

Will the gaps widen with the years?
Do you know the day my grandmother died was hot, baking?
Can you tell I like sex from the back row?

I'd like it now, on this black chair that you move
up or down, bringing me back to life
telling me in a cheerful voice, I'm done.

Jackie Kay

Part 7

Inner Self and Imagination

Green Thought

Stealthy as any unicorn he
drops his capsule among the books:
knowing that unreason, like ink, runs
the more you rub at it.

Inexpungeable, alert, with muddied fingers
poised like a chef's, he
sows the brilliant flowers
that hedge the child's dreams

and pout in the dreams
of her parents. The readers sleep.
Poetry jumps from her shelf
and stalks into the moonlight:

she's the songster and the bloodied
shroud. Our heroine
clenches her hand to the bedhead again:
sweet Jack, nimble Jack's come calling.

Fiona Sampson

1

The Unborn

The queen in her garden
Walked through the high grass
And found an infant prince
In an egg of blue glass.

Not the sun's down feathers
In that deep green nest,
Nor the warmth of the queen's arms,
Nor the heat of her breast,

Could awaken that child
Which sleeping lay
In his blue ice-coffin
At bright mid-day.

Gerda Mayer

Sculpting the light

At dawn I create you, again.
From a swathe of air
I shape the curve of your spine
with the palm of my hand,
my fingertips scoop a gulley
for the base of your neck,
smooth a hollow, a place to linger
in the small of your back.

Keeping you is like trying to touch
crystals of frost.
You glow for a moment, lit by the sun.
In the melt of dawn
another bed stands in the mirror
and in it a woman, waking alone.

Jill Eulalie Dawson

Dark Mothers

Gazing at shadows on a summer curtain.
Knowing that, behind, the sun is rising.

Because I am half asleep,
between me and the sun her plaster head
is a shadow watching at the sill, tilt
of nose and chin, lips opening,
a living mother come to waken.
And I am a child in cool bedclothes.

All night I have wrestled, too hot, too cold,
with old age coming fast, the brain
humming with tension on stiff shoulders.
Now everything's flowing again,
the skin eases on the blood, bones
stop drying to skeleton, are suddenly
rocks awash with gleaming salt.

Past them and out over the wave's curve
(towards where mind listens) the coo-roo-coo
of a pigeon binds me to the wild wood,
the gnarl of hollow trunks still growing.
Their pith's the film of brain in a skull
misconceived but working. Flushes of thought
wrap in colour the scan's dark void, line
the chalice of bone whose wide eyes
can still see.
            In mine, an after-image
of my mother's head is changing
to lines of older heritage, coiled
in uneasy dreams, where blood and bone
spiral from the sperm, spilling molecules,
shaping the changes. The sun is young
that saw them beginning. It casts an image
on our drawn blinds – the Dark Mother
of past and future jungles. The tilt
of her brain lifts blind eyes
to horizons invisible.
                    No straight line
draws us beyond the coming deaths,
humankind's, the earth's, our own,
but – as the human hand illuminates
spirals from leaf through word to nondescript –
the sun could craft a becoming, our branch
arrowed from life-tree to open margin.

Just now, a mere half-century holds me
woven into sun and shade, half dreaming
under open windows. There is a chorus
of shorter lives, buzzing and chirping shadows,
a silent drift of butterflies and leaves
and, seeking entry at the curtain's slit,
ginger mog, my angular black Anubis.

Anne Cluysenaar

Glose: Water and Stone

I am a woman sixty years old and of no special courage.
Everyday – a little conversation with God, or his envoy
*   the tall pine, or the grass-swimming cricket.*
Everyday – I study the difference between water and stone.
Everyday – I stare at the world; I push the grass aside
*   and stare at the world.*
                    'Work': Mary Oliver

As I drive over a body of land on a ribbon
of tarmac west from Fishguard there's a wolf's castle
of rocks against a sky so wide, so unbroken
that I think for an instant of what I bring, scars
where a breast lived, neck held with a pin, seven
(at least) of my nine lives gone. But this damage
may mend – and light in high places is vast
and unfolds, nameless, like something given.
Most like a sexual pang, a silent pledge:
I am a woman sixty years old and of no special courage.

Stacked in uneven layers, accretions of heat
shimmer above a field and corral horses
in a small group under sheltering alder trees
too far away to see, but I imagine water,
leaves mouthing over a muddy stream,
breeze and breath – God doesn't come into it –
the horses stock still, while straw-coloured stalks
of cow-parsley sway under spread loads of seeds,
packed seed-heads whispering their dry secrets
to the tall pine or the grass-swimming cricket.

Motionless, the estuary today, brim-full
and monochrome; each grass-blade mirrors
itself in perfect symmetry, each white gull
floats on its own double. Even the kingfishers
are paired – in air, not water – flying parallel
to the path, two black specks until they turn
under the bridge and there's a flash of blue brighter
than toffee-paper, a miracle as small and usual
as stone breaking water, water polishing stone.
Everyday I study the difference between water and stone.

I'd like to think that part of what I see
when I gaze at the world – those stopped moments
when the breath is knocked away – might be
imprinted on my chromosomes. Then, once
my ninth and last life fails, the cells finally
close and all the atoms disperse, I'll meld
with specks of stone and grass, become fragments
in the dust particulate spinning daily
from dark to light to dark. Sixty years old:
I push the grass aside and stare at the world.

Mary MacRae

Multiplying the Moon

No opening in the house is shut
but the heat's a cage I have to bear.
By the back door where I burnt
my soles this afternoon I long for air

cool as a fish's belly to creep out
of Pymmes Brook up the park slope
to my fence, press the milky smell
of midnight blades to my face. Not

a ruffle, not even the owl
calling like an obsessive ghost
from clots of trees. Upstairs the curtains
are undrawn and I watch my self in a mist

of cotton nightdress that hides scars,
uneven troughs, veins that have discoloured
skin with spidery purple tributaries.
And there are my other selves, stars

for eyes, leaning towards the windows:
the one with drive who hoards hope,
the limp moaner, the sympathetic self
and she whose glinting thoughts leap

from the dark of her riverbed. None
of these can lower the temperature,
slow or speed up time, shrink hatreds
fostered for centuries, feed rain

to thirsty fields, muzzle the snout
of danger or make safe the small
creature always crouched at my core.
Powerless then, have I no power at all?

Pushing a pane to its limit, I catch
the moon. Across the window bay
a second jumps whitely into
the blue of night. In the glass I hatch

another and another, bat them from frame
to frame, create a skyful of moons,
ring myself with silver clarity. Cool
begins to whisker the rim of the room.

Myra Schneider

The Value of X

Some nights I'm obliged to go down once more
by the light of my skin, fingers testing
diagonals and verticals, toes curled
over the treads, to seek out
the nub of the lamp and startle it
onto a gallery of objects

just to check on her: and yes, there she is,
unfinished as ever, blocked face sleepless hair
boxed in the cube of window glass;
and we stare at each other, two halves
of an equation, still at a loss
how to deduce the value of X.

M. R. Peacocke

Fox on the Stairs

Feral as the sun's chestnut stain,
slipping like ruby glass,
fox leaves her spoor on every tread,
gilt spraints down each riser.

She wants me to follow,
though I can't catch her,
past the blazing pale of the banisters,
onto the landing's gilded and distressed field.

Wild as best blue milk, fox milk,
sharp as dextrose spiking my blood,
she wants me crazy, bright teeth fastened
in my heart with a wilderness clasp.

No emblem, she trots, tongue lolling,
up the vertebral column of the house,
past each blue eyelid shuttered room,
bright as a needle through folded shadow.

Her musk paints the air impasto
and I will never bleach it clean
or feel the house like a newly
bathed domestic animal, settle.

Kate Foley

The Woman who Dreamed of Eels

She is ankle-deep in water,
I'm in the sea, she thinks, then remembers
she's asleep. When they push against her

like cats demanding love,
their faces all snout, heads bobbing,
she knows it's the eel dream again.

She tries to grab them,
just like last night, brings her hand up
empty, smells brine, something gone off.

If I can interpret the dream
while dreaming, they'll go away
and I'll wake up.

So she thinks hard about eels,
dead ones, swimming in liquor,
served at the pie shop.

Just then they fill her mouth,
sour, still alive. She tries to scream
but the eels make her gag.

She wakes, remembers nothing.
There's a strange coating
on her tongue.

Tamar Yoseloff

The Badge

Finding myself after nights of grief and dread
in a room full of rainy light
knife in my hand, no-one can do this for me,
I prepare for the ceremony

I am about the join the community
of those who have removed and replaced their heads.

Cutting it off is easy, I feel no pain,
what's difficult is finding the thing again
wherever on the carpet it's rolled to.

Headless, but I see with shadow-sight
a fluid shudder of colours, images
which will soon falter and disintegrate
unless I reattach my head quickly

and I must do it quickly, it's not too late
while nerves and flesh are still living.

I'm trembling cold and bright
as a knife-edge, I feel high
and light as you do when shrugging off a pack
you've slogged under for miles. And there

on the floor it lies, I recognise the hair
tumbled and black, the face
turned mercifully aside, a glimpse of cheek and brow

that's mine all right so I take it
lift it like a warm and weighty stone
up to my neck and steady it in place.

I must wait now while vein and bone
and fibres knit together
motionless in case it all untethers
as round me the others gather

praising, giving me space. Thin fluid
oozes from the join – is this normal? They nod
yes, yes, don't worry, it's healing.

My lover wants to hug me, and I say no
not yet, this is still too new

but he leads me to a seat beneath the window
plump with purple cushions, he kisses me
and promises he won't disturb my head

which balances on its stem
like a flower just opened.

As he enters me I touch my neck
very softly and think of the scar I'll have,
the badge of those who've lost their heads and regained them

a fine red necklace, indelible thread.

Hilary Llewellyn-Williams

2

Porphyria

She's a Cover Girl. An Italian beauty
on the front of a glossy magazine —
yet she's been around for two thousand years,
her skull full of dust, sealed in a sea-wall.

Now jets of water pour from her eyes —
she's cleansed, photographed, catalogued.
They call her Porphyria, take her gold rings,
the bracelets she's been guarding with her bones
since A.D. 79. Her skeleton speaks secrets
to scientists; the biographical bones reveal
no babies, but the elongated arms of a weaver,
hard-working, with perfect teeth, aquiline nose
and her left fibula fractured near the knee —
probably in a childhood fall.

Stripped of her gold, she's her own jewellery:
the pale chain of spine and torcs of ribs,
circlet of pelvis and casket-cranium holding
centuries, the stored sea-sounds of a shell.

What of her soul's secrets, lost
in lava? Troubles, leaving no imprint –
not even shadow-shapes in sand.
Or the love her eyes conveyed; caresses
with her supple weaver's fingers
of the giver of the rings. And her flesh —
the sun of twenty summers on her arms,
salt of the dark blue Tyrrhenian Sea,
oil of the olive and oleander blossom.
But the flesh's truth and the bone's truth
are not the same. Our minds can search
for hers: the bones won't tell.

Gladys Mary Coles

Bridal Path

The worst time of the year
For such a long journey: early November snow
And the horses straining through the drifts.
From the frontier royal guards escorted them.
They reached their destination ten days late.

She was sixteen and had never seen the sea.
In the darkness the waves crashed.
Then lights and a fire to roast an ox
In the castle hall
And the chattering died away.

She clutched her fur cloak round her.
Two men rose from chairs by a map-strewn table
Near the fire and came towards her.
"Oh God," she prayed, "Let it be him,
The young one with the golden hair."

When they reached her, he stood back,
The young one. "God give you joy, brother."
The one with the grizzled beard, the sword-ripped cheek,
The piercing eyes that hardly saw her,
Took and kissed her hand.

"Welcome to Elsinore, my Lady Gertrude."

Alison Pryde

Settlement

He came in early summer
that first time
riding a sway-backed mare.

Father called off the dogs
and cap in hand
bent his ear to new words.

The mare lifted her lip
to the fresh green, grazing
among the naked ewes.

Wind lifted the washed wool.
Mother hit the comb from my hand
for stopping to look.

I stared through my hair
my hand loosing the knots
from the curled fleece

teasing the burrs free
until a strand came clear
to pull through the card.

He looked at me once
took in the filled fields
weighed up the wool.

Mother fetched ale and bread.
There was silence and talk.
Later they shook hands.

Pat Corina

Her Women 1463-1489

And now to business;
one kneels to the linen chest, raises the lid
for swaddling, one fills a shallow dish,
one spreads towels, one dabbles water with her fingertips.

Two conspire. Two console her, offer her the child.
But what concerns her here is what's outside
the curtained door, what comes after.
Nothing more, they tell her, *nothing worse*.

One wipes the hefty wooden secateurs
one drags a sodden mop, two bundle sheets
and rags, one tends the stove. One leaves
and comes back with the priest.

Ann Sansom

The Falconer's Bride

Before the hawking party
you stroked the falcon's breast
with a little switch;

showed me the immature plumage,
transparent hunger-traces on the welts,
the shafts still full of blood.

It was a skill you said
to keep a hawk from sleeping,
marry its speed with the wind.

I have embroidered lure and hood with noble metals;
cut from supple leather
the sliding-jesses worn even in flight.

You gave me the white gyrfalcon in Lent;
but today, I remembered
how you filled your mouth with water,

sprayed it through closed lips
onto the restive bird's breast –
and her sudden pure mantling.

Pauline Stainer

Lady with the Unicorn

Musée du Moyen Age, Paris

For years they've kept her here
in darkness with her bowl of sweets,
her portable organ, her careful crown of flowers

under this artificial moon
to live out her sentence in an embroidered field
of lilies, tasting the intricate fruit

while through her looking-glass
he admires himself, the slowly emerging shape
of a perfect stallion at grass.

Now he stands and waits.
She strokes his horn, and his ears go goatish,
his muzzle elongates.

Is there no end? The stoat, the fox, the heron,
the monkey with wicked eyes
remember another time

before they were brought here, torn
and threadbare, when a tide of rot
rose through the stitches of the horn

like water round a marker, till only her hand
flowered on the pale tip
under the crescents of her flag,

around her the bowl and circlet bobbing,
the animals one by one,
the organ chiming as the waves came in.

Susan Wicks

3

Aubergine

Nothing is more beautiful
than this aubergine,
a musk of purple sheen
scented with earth
as it lay pregnant on straw.
Its green calyx still hugs
the great and gorgeous bulge.

I placed it
on an orange plate,
on a brown table.
All day I have come
to look, to touch,
to stroke.

Ayatollah Khomeini warned the maidens
this fruit from Eden
could tempt them to immodest thoughts.
How wrong the Ayatollah.
Aubergine is a gravid woman,
a queen, her skin licked satin,
her colour arousal.

Patricia Bishop

Willow Creek

The janitor came out of his eely cave
and said 'Your mother was a good swimmer.
Go back and tell her it's not yet time.'

Were there no other animals in Eden?
When she dives under the roots, I thought,
an eel is the last shape she'll want to meet.

Her brother was the one for eels: farm-wise,
ruthless about food. You roll the skin back
and pull it off inside out like a stocking.

He grew up with dogs, horses and cattle.
She was more at home with water and music;
there were several lives for her after the creek.

In one of them she taught my younger son
to swim in the Greek sea; and walked through Athens
under a parasol, to buy us melon.

Fruit for the grandchildren; nectarines and pears
for the great-grandchildren; feijoa-parties...
'There's more of that to come,' said the janitor.

'But no more swimming. Remember how she plunged
into a hotel pool in bra and knickers,
rather than miss the chance? She must have been sixty.'

I had some questions for the janitor,
but he submerged himself under the willows
in his cavern where I couldn't follow –

you have to be invited; I wasn't, yet,
and neither was she. Meanwhile, she's been allowed
a rounded segment of something warm and golden:

not pomegranate, paw-paw. She used to advise
eating the seeds; a few of them, with the fruit,
were good for you in some way – I forget.

Long life, perhaps. She knows about these things.
And she won't let a few eels bother her.
She's tougher than you might think, my mother.

Fleur Adcock

Taking it in

About cuckoo-time in the bit of copse
she warned my shadow. Clap of my heart
startled both our skins. While I stood prickling
she mapped me with her tongue.

The babble and challenge of the morning
fell to a breath. I became a tree
and the sun had time to spread on the bank
while she assessed my heat.

As we grew softer to one another
she showed me her belly distended
with children, narrow godlets, and drew them
over the oakleaf crumb

without haste towards some brackeny dark
and vanished. Birdsong streamed back. The light
she had worn like a membrane found its place
on leaves and beads of grit.

She left no trace but in my head. Tell me,
Maker of serpents, how many lives
I shall need to swallow the whole world's egg
without spilling a drop.

M. R. Peacocke

The Lady and the Hare

They would have you believe
she slept on bedrock
where ash roots the stone

that what startled silence
was not a buzzard mewing
but the huntsman's horn unblown.

When the hounds
broke from their thicket
they froze at her calm

sensed in the cold apse
of her breast
both the dove and the bone.

Today we started no hare;
downstream of the waterfall
found only her shrine

and how sternly
the warm hare is folded
inside her fierce gown.

Pauline Stainer

The Mermaid Pew in Zennor Church, Cornwall

She bends her tail in balance with the pew,
wide-breasted girl, entangling the church.

Her belly shines where fishermen have touched
with rope-singed hands the round umbilicus.

The carver dug each nipple from the grain
and separated out two sturdy fins.

He chiselled gifts she holds up in both hands,
the mirror and the comb in truthful oak.

Half fish, half girl, she symbolises Christ
whose dual nature tethers souls to heaven.

And both claimed lives, singing out their promises:
'Let down your nets and I will give you love'.

He walked on water, certain of his bearings
but, flowing with the tides, she is the sea.

Jill Bamber

At Sychar

St. John 4: 5-42

Now Jacob's well was there

and what was surprising was that he spoke to her,

that he tested the truthfulness in her,

a woman of Samaria,

frail as the world or the waterpot she would leave there,

that he tasted the truth in her, like water.

Gillian Allnutt

Yashoda's Vision

Krishna, barely past crawling on all fours,
full of a child's curiosity and love,
eager to devour the world –

is one day accused of eating dirt.
His playmates complain to Yashoda,
Krishna's foster mother,
who unable to ignore matters further
is forced to chide her charge; she commands
Krishna to reveal the contents of his mouth.

As she kneels to peer inside this cavern,
she witnesses the birth of the universe –
the sun, moon, stars, galaxies,
the oceans, earth, deserts, volcanoes,
animals and plants long extinct,
time, love, death, birth, pain, wisdom, ecstasy;
not a life, leaf, stone, word, person missing.

Yashoda sees herself, all her past
incarnations, with all the dirt, the dust
of the universe in its place; for a moment
blessed with insight, the essence of Creation…

Shanta Acharya

An Angel

After a long drive west into Wales,
as I lay on my bed, waiting
for my mind to seep back through my body,
I watched two gothic panels draw apart.
Between them loomed an angel,
tall as a caryatid, wingless,
draped like Michelangelo's sibyl.
Never have I felt so profoundly looked into.

She was bracing on her hip an immense book
that at first I took for a Bible. Then
prickling consciousness seemed to apprehend
The Recording Angel.
The pen she wielded writhed like a caduceus,
and on the book
ECCE LIBER MORI had been branded.

This book she held out towards me,
arm-muscles tensing, but even as I reached
I knew it was too heavy to hold.
Its gravity, she made me feel, would crush me,
a black hole of infinitely compressed time.
Each page weighed as much as the world.

Drawing my attention to a flaw in the book's crust –
a glazed porthole, a lens of alizarin –
she focused it (it must have been a microscope)
and silently motioned me to look.
Fire folding fire was all I saw. Then the red glass
cleared and a blizzard of swimming cells
swept underneath it, lashing their whip-like tails,
clashing, fusing, consuming each other greedily,
fountaining into polyps and underwater flowers.
Soon – fast-forward – forests were shooting up.
Seasons tamed lagoons of bubbling mud
where, hatching from the scum, animalculae
crawled, swarmed, multiplied, disbanded,
swarmed again, raised cities out of dust,
destroyed them, died. I turned to the angel,
'Save these species,' I cried.
And brought my face right down on her book,
my cheek on the lens like a lid.

Instantly I knew I had put out a light
that had never been generated by a book.
That vision-furnace, that blink into genesis?
Nothing but a passing reflection of the angel.

Rising, for the first time afraid,
I confronted her immortality
circling like a bracelet of phosphorus
just outside the windscreen of the car.
For it seems I was still driving.
Solidity and substance disappeared.
A noose of frenzied, shimmering electrons,
motes of an approaching migraine,
closed around me.
And through that fluorescent manacle,
the road flowed on through Wales.

Anne Stevenson

203

from: Entries on Light

Everywhere you see her, who could have been
   Monet's woman with a parasol
who's no woman at all but an excuse for wind –
   passage of light-and-shade we know
wind by – just as his pond was no pond
   but a globe at his feet turning to show
how the liquid, dry, go topsy-turvy, how far
   sky goes down in water. Like iris, agapanthus
waterplants from margins where, tethered
   by their cloudy roots, clouds grow underwater
and lily-floes, like landing-craft, hover
   waiting for departure, she comes at a slant
to crosswinds, currents, against shoals of sunlight
   set adrift, loans you her reflection.
I saw her the other day I don't know where
   at a tangent to some evening, to a sadness
she never shares. She wavers, like recognition.
   Something of yours goes through her, something
of hers escapes. To hillbrows, meadows
   where green jumps into her skirt, hatbrim shadows
blind her. To coast, wind at her heels, on diagonals
   as the minute hand on the hour, the hour
on the wheel of sunshades. Everywhere you see her.
   On beaches, bramble paths, terraces of Edwardian
hotels. In antique shops, running her thumb along
   napworn velvet. A nail buffer. An owl brooch
with two black eyes of onyx. Eyes she fingers.
   But usually on a slope. Coming your way.

Mimi Khalvati

Acknowledgements

The poems in this anthology are reprinted from the following books, all by permission of the publishers listed or of the poet where copyright rests solely with the poet. Thanks are due to all the copyright holders cited below for their kind permission.

Shanta Acharya: Yashoda's Vision, *Looking In, Looking Out* (Headland, 2005).
Anna Adams: Unrecorded Speech 1, *Nobodies* (Peterloo Poets, 2002);
      Knocking On, *Flying Underwater* (Peterloo Poets, 2004).
Fleur Adcock: Witnesses; Willow Creek; both poems from
      Collected Poems 1960-2000 (Bloodaxe Books, 2000).
Kim Addonizio: "What Do Women Want?", *Tell Me* (BOA Editions, USA, 2000).
Patience Agbabi: The Wife of Bafa, *Transformatrix* (Payback Press, 2000).
Ann Alexander: Four women wed, *Facing Demons* (Peterloo Poets, 2002).
Gillian Allnutt: The Widow's Mite, Effie, Dumfries, 1916; German Woman,
      1945; both poems from *Sojourner* (Bloodaxe Books, 2004).
Moniza Alvi: The Thieves, *How the Stone Found Its Voice* (Bloodaxe Books, 2005).
R. V. Bailey: With You, *Marking Time* (Peterloo Poets, 2004).
Judith Barrington: Larks, *Trying To Be An Honest Woman* (The Eighth Mountain
      Press, 1985).
Elizabeth Bartlett: Birth; Quite a Day; Smile for Daddy; all poems from *Two
      Women Dancing: New and Selected Poems* (Bloodaxe Books, 1995).
Alice Beer: Willendorf Venus, *Talking of Pots, People and Points of View*
      (poetry pf, 2005).
Denise Bennett: Black Shells, *American Dresses* (Flarestack, 2000).
Anne Beresford: What do you do all day when I'm at school?, *No Place for
      Cowards* (Katabasis, 1998).
Elizabeth Bewick: Heartsease, *Heartsease* (Peterloo Poets, 1991).
Patricia Bishop: Saving Dragons, *Saving Dragons* (Oversteps Books, 2000).
Pat Borthwick: Scan, *Swim* (Mudfog, 2005); Katya, *Monkey Puzzles* (Pharos
      Press, 1996).
Sara Boyes: Romantic Notions, *Black Flame* (Hearing Eye, 2005).
Jean Binta Breeze: Moon, *The Arrival of Bright Eye* (Bloodaxe Books, 2000).
Carole Bromley: Thomas, *Unscheduled Halt* (Smith / Doorstop Books, 2004).
Jacqueline Brown: Anorectic, *Fractured Flights* (Arc Publications, 2002);
      Poaching, *Thinking Egg* (Littlewood Arc, 1993).
Catherine Byron: Allowing the Animal; The Blue Darkness; both poems from
      The Getting of Vellum (Blackwater Press, 2000; Salmon Publishing, Ireland,
      2000); Let-Down, *The Fat Hen Field Hospital* (Loxwood Stoneleigh, 1993).
Linda Chase: Formerly, *The Wedding Spy* (Bloodaxe Books, 2001).
Alison Chisholm: Miss Jenkins' Lesson, *Daring the Slipstream* (Headland, 1997).
Gillian Clarke: The Hare, *Collected Poems, 1997* (Carcanet Press, 1997).
Anne Cluysenaar: Dark Mothers, *Timeslips, New and Selected Poems* (Carcanet
      Press, 1997).
Gladys Mary Coles: Porphyria, *The Glass Island* (Duckworth, 1992 and 1994).

Merle Collins: Sometimes in the Morning, *Lady in a Boat* (Peepal Tree Press, 2003).

Ann Drysdale: Thinking of you, *Between Dryden and Duffy* (Peterloo Poets, 2005).

Carol Ann Duffy: Warming Her Pearls, *Selling Manhattan* (Anvil Press Poetry, 1987).

Jane Duran: Zagharit; Dementia; both poems from *Coastal* (Enitharmon Press, 2005).

Ruth Fainlight: Sheba and Solomon, Part 1, Their Words; Essential Equipment; both poems from *Burning Wire* (Bloodaxe Books, 2002).

U A Fanthorpe: Women Laughing; Maud Speaking; Mother Scrubbing the Floor; Atlas; all poems from *Collected Poems 1978-2003* (Peterloo Poets, 2005).

Vicki Feaver: Women's Blood, *The Handless Maiden* (Cape, 1994).

Elaine Feinstein: Photographs; The White Bird; both poems from *Collected Poems and Translations* (Carcanet Press, 2002).

Janet Fisher: Women Who Dye Their Hair, *Women Who Dye Their Hair* (Smith / Doorstop Books, 2001).

Rose Flint: The Rigger's Wife, *Blue Horse of Morning* (Seren Books, 1991).

Kate Foley: Tall Foreign Doctor; Do You Like Chocolate?; Fox on the Stairs; all poems from *A Year Without Apricots* (Blackwater Press, 1999).

Linda France: Homage to My Latin Teacher, *The Simultaneous Dress* (Bloodaxe Books, 2003).

Wendy French: Graffiti; When the Waters Break; both poems from *Splintering the Dark* (Rockingham Press, 2005).

Cynthia Fuller: Boy, Part 1; Ghosts; both poems from *Instructions for the Desert* (Flambard, 1996).

Katherine Gallagher: Hunger; Distances; both poems from *Tigers on the Silk Road* (Arc Publications, 2000).

Rhian Gallagher: Shine, *Salt Water Creek* (Enitharmon Press, 2003).

Rebecca Goss: The Night My Father Died, a version of the poem published as 'Mother' in *Keeping Houston Time* (Slow Dancer Press, 1997).

Anne Grimes: Mother and Daughter, *Alice's Cat* (Peterloo Poets, 2003).

Cathy Grindrod: Secret, *Fighting Talk* (Headland 2005).

Rita Ann Higgins: Some People, *Sunny Side Plucked* (Bloodaxe Books, 1996).

Selima Hill: I am hers and she is mine, *Violet* (Bloodaxe Books, 1997).

Helen Ivory: Gone, *The Dog in the Sky* (Bloodaxe Books, 2006).

Martha Kapos: Mute, *My Nights in Cupid's Palace* (Enitharmon Press, 2003).

Judith Kazantzis: A Photograph Seen When I Was Twelve, *Swimming Through the Grand Hotel* (Enitharmon Press, 1997).

Jackie Kay: The Black Chair, *Off Colour* (Bloodaxe Books, 1998).

Mimi Khalvati: Staring up from his pram to the sky, Everywhere you see her, *Entries on Light* (Carcanet Press, 1997).

Jane Kinninmont: Children's Ward, *Seven League Stilettos* (Ragged Raven Poetry, 2004).

Angela Kirby: Remedial Action; Graffiti (a version of the original published poem); both poems from *Mr Irresistible* (Shoestring Press, 2005).

Pauline Kirk: Visit to the Museum (a version of the original poem) published in *Rights of Way* (Unibird Press, 1990) and *Walking to Snailbeach, Selected and New Poems* (Redbeck Press, 2004).

Lotte Kramer: Signing Him Away, *The Desecration of Trees* (Hippopotamus Press,1994); For Bread – 1920s, *The Phantom House* (Rockingham Press, 2000); Lena, our maid, *Selected and New Poems 1980–1997* (Rockingham Press, 1997).

Stevie Krayer: Flood: IV, *Voices from A Burning Boat* (Poetry Salzburg, 1997).

Dinah Livingstone: Bluebells, *Presence* (Katabasis, 2003).

Hilary Llewellyn-Williams: The Badge, *Greenland* (Seren, 2003).

Kathleen McPhilemy: Mothers, *The Lion in the Forest* (Katabasis, 2004).

Gerda Mayer: The Old Worcester Women, *A Heartache of Grass* (Peterloo Poets, 1988); The Unborn, *Monkey On The Analyst's Couch* (Ceolfrith Press, 1980).

Paula Meehan: The Ghost of My Mother Comforts Me; Not Your Muse; both poems from *Pillow Talk* (The Gallery Press, 1994); My Sister Lets Down Her Hair, *Dharmakaya* (Carcanet Press, 1980).

Geraldine Messenbird-Smith: Grandma Makes a Spitfire – Grandma Wins the War, *The Ticking Crocodile* (Blinking Eye Publishing, 2004).

Lyn Moir: Not exactly a David, *Breakers' Yard* (Arrowhead Press, 2003).

Esther Morgan: Bone China; Growing a Girl; both poems from *The Silence Living in Houses* (Bloodaxe Books, 2005).

Caroline Natzler: Colouring In, *Design Fault* (Flambard Press, 2001).

Mandy Pannett: Erma's Search (a version of the original published poem); The Hammer Stone; both poems from *Bee Purple* (Oversteps Books, 2002).

M. R. Peacocke: Taking It In, *Speaking of the Dead* (Peterloo Poets, 2003).

Pascale Petit: The Magma Room, *The Zoo Father* (Seren, 2001); My Mother's Perfume, *The Huntress* (Seren, 2005).

Patricia Pogson: Women's Medical, *A Crackle from the Larder* (Redbeck Press, 1991).

Caroline Price: Morning Sickness; Pictures Against Skin; both poems from *Pictures Against Skin* (Rockingham Press, 1994).

Pauline Prior-Pitt: The Visit, *Ironing with Sue Lawley* (Spike Press, 2005).

Alison Pryde: Bridal Path, *Have we had Easter yet?* (Peterloo Poets, 1998).

Lesley Quayle: The Killer Woman, *A Perfect Spit At The Stars* (Spanna in the Works, 1999).

Elisabeth Rowe: Last Wish, *In Love* (Leaf Books, 2006).

Anne Ryland: Fire Child, a version of the poem published in *Autumnologist* (Arrowhead Press, 2006).

Fiona Sampson: Green Thought, *Folding the Real* (Seren, 2001).

Maureen Sangster: In The Fish-House, *Out of the Urn* (Scottish Contemporary Poets Series, Scottish Cultural Press, 1997).

Ann Sansom: Princess, *Romance* (Bloodaxe Books,1994); Nancy; Her Women 1463-1489, *In Praise of Men and Other People* (Bloodaxe Books, 2003).

Carole Satyamurti: Broken Moon; Piccadilly Line; both poems from *Stitching the Dark: New and Selected Poems* (Bloodaxe Books, 2005).

Maggie Sawkins: Charcot's Pet, *Charcot's Pet* (Flarestack, 2002).

Myra Schneider: Yellow, *Insisting on Yellow, New and Selected Poems* (Enitharmon Press, 2000); Amazon; Multiplying the Moon; both poems from *Multiplying the Moon* (Enitharmon Press, 2004).

Mary Sheepshanks: Working Out, *Dancing Blues to Skylarks* (Fighting Cock Press, 2004).

Penelope Shuttle: Vanity, *A Leaf Out of His Book* (Oxford / Carcanet Press, 1999); Outgrown, *Selected Poems* (OUP, 1998).

Nicola Slee: The Fathers, a short version of the poem published in *Praying Like A Woman* (SPCK, 2004).

Joan Jobe Smith: The Pow Wow Café, *The Pow Wow Café* (Smith / Doorstop Books, 1998).

Margaret Speak: The Firefly Cage, *The Firefly Cage* (Redbeck Press, 1998).

Jean Sprackland: Deadnettle, *Tattoos for Mothers' Day* (Spike Press, 1997).

Pauline Stainer: The Ringing Chamber; The Lady and the Hare; The Falconer's Bride; all poems from *The Lady & The Hare* (Bloodaxe Books, 2003).

Anne Stevenson: Poem for a Daughter; Lost; An Angel; all poems from *Poems 1955-2005* (Bloodaxe Books, 2005).

Isobel Thrilling: The Headmistress, *The Chemistry of Angels* (halfacrown press, 2000); from Mother, *Spectrum Shift* (Littlewood, 1991).

Susan Utting: The Florist's Assistant, *Striptease* (Smith / Doorstop Books, 2001).

Fiona Ritchie Walker: Filling the Kettle, *Garibaldi's Legs* (Iron Press, 2005).

Sarah Wardle: Full Moon with My Grandmother, *Fields Away* (Bloodaxe Books, 2003).

Frances Wilson: Coming of Age, *Close to Home* (Rockingham Press, 1993).

Lynne Wycherley: Coming of Age, *At the Edge of Light* (Shoestring Press, 2003); For the Shetland Lace-knitters, *North Flight* (Shoestring Press 2006).

Tamar Yoseloff: Partobar; The Woman Who Dreamed of Eels; both poems from *Barnard's Star* (Enitharmon Press, 2004).

COVER SCULPTURE:
Mirror by Pascale Petit (1984)
from the exhibition Pandora's Box,
Women's Images of Women.
Photograph by Cath Tate.

About Second Light

Second Light Network (SLN) is a group of some 350 women poets aged 40+ with associate membership open to younger women. It supports and promotes women's poetry through publications, readings, workshops and an annual residential workshop at Launde Abbey in Leicestershire. SLN has co-operated with established poetry publishers to issue 3 anthologies of women's poetry, of which *Images of Women* is the latest. *Parents* was published by Enitharmon (2000, Editors: Myra Schneider and Dilys Wood) and *Making Worlds* by Headland (2003, Editors: Gladys Mary Coles, Myra Schneider and Dilys Wood). Second Light Publishing has issued *Four Caves of the Heart* (2004, Editors: Myra Schneider and Caroline Price) and *My Mother Threw Knives* (2006, Editors: Wendy French, Maggie Sawkins and Dilys Wood). *My Mother Threw Knives* is twinned with *Images of Women* but focusses on the work of up and coming women poets. Details of SLN and how to join may be obtained from Dilys Wood, 9 Greendale Close, London SE22 8TG. e-mail: dilyswood@tiscali.co.uk

About the Editors

Myra Schneider's most recent books are *Insisting on Yellow, New and Selected Poems* (Enitharmon, 2000), *Writing My Way Through Cancer* (Jessica Kingsley, 2003) and *Multiplying the Moon* (Enitharmon, 2004). She is co-editor with John Killick of *Writing for Self discovery* (Element Books, 1998) and has written fiction for children and teenagers. She is co-editor of four collections of women's poetry. She works as a tutor for the Poetry School and is consultant to the Second Light Network.

Dilys Wood founded the Second Light Network in 1994. Her Collection is *Women Come to a Death* (Katabasis, 1997).